Outside

First edition 2014
Text copyright © Maria Ana Peixe Dias and Inês Teixeira do Rosário
Illustrations copyright © Bernardo P. Carvalho

Published with the permission of Planeta Tangerina
Rua das Rosas, n.° 20, Alto dos Lombos, 2775-683 Carcavelos, Portugal

Funded by the Dirção-Geral do Livro, dos Arquivos e das Bibliotecas/Portugal

GOVERNO DE PORTUGAL | SECRETÁRIO DE E DA CULTURA

DIREÇÃO-GERAL DO LIVRO, DOS ARQUIV
DAS BIBLIOTECAS

First published in Great Britain in 2016 by Frances Lincoln Children's Books,
74-77 White Lion Street, London N1 9PF
QuartoKnows.com
Visit our blogs at QuartoKnows.com

A catalogue record for this book is available from the British Library.

ISBN 978-1-84780-769-4

Designed by Planeta Tangerina
Translated by Lucy Greaves
Original edition edited by Isabel Minhós Martins and Carlos Grifo Babo
English language edition edited by Jenny Broom

Natural history consultancy:
Ana Francisco, Sérgio Chozas and Paulo Cardoso – SPBotânica ("Flowers")
Maria João Pereira ("Mammals")
Mário Boieiro (animals and "Bugs and Critters")
Miguel Lecoq, Paulo Catry, Ricardo Tomé ("Birds")
Nuno Pedroso ("Follow The Clues" and "Mammals")
Ricardo Calado ("Beaches, Oceans, and Tidepools")
Rui Rebelo ("Amphibeans" and "Reptiles")
Sónia Antón ("The Stars, the Moon and the Sun")
Teresa Leal Rosa ("Clouds, Wind and Rain")
Teresa Melo ("Rocks")

Printed in China

9 8 7 6 5 4 3 2 1

OUTSIDE

A GUIDE TO DISCOVERING NATURE

Maria Ana Peixe Dias

Inês Teixeira Do Rosário

Bernardo P. Carvalho

Translated by Lucy Greaves

Frances Lincoln
Children's Books

Us and nature . . . a long story

Imagine people in prehistoric times, before there were villages or cities. Nature was all around them! Back then, there were no paved roads, no houses, and no electricity. There were plains stretching as far as the eye could see, rivers running freely, huge mountains and cliffs, lots of animal species (buzzing or growling ferociously), and trees and more trees.

For thousands and thousands of years, it was just us and nature.

And, in fact, there was no real separation—us on one side; plants, animals, and rivers on the other. We were so close because we depended on the natural world to survive: we needed the fruits and berries that grew on the trees; the fish that swam in the rivers and seas; the animals, large and small, that we hunted on land.

Nature was mysterious. We were starting to figure some things out, but still, everything happened as if by magic. (And there are so many mysteries left to solve today, so just imagine what it must have been like back then . . .)

Nature was also powerful. No one could hold back a raging river by force. There was no way to predict a storm. There weren't any inventions to help with farming.

Nature was a friend, but also an enemy. Imagine what it would be like to live surrounded by animals that wanted to eat you! Or what it would be like to live through hard winters, droughts, floods, and diseases that could destroy the plants you needed to eat. That's why, at the beginning, we prayed to the mountains, the trees, and the rivers. Nature was like a living person, or like a god that people could talk to and ask for things from or offer a gift to in exchange for a big favor.

Hail to thee, O Nile!
Thou showest thyself in this land,
Coming in peace, giving life to Egypt!

The ancient Egyptians used to sing this hymn to the Nile River.

Giving life to all animals;
Watering the land without ceasing:
The way of heaven descending:
Lover of food, bestower of corn.

Unpredictability has always scared us. The ancient Egyptians, for example, could never be sure whether or not the flooding of the Nile would water the earth and give them fertile ground. Throughout our history, the need to survive (in this case, to eat!) made us want to control nature and its forces.

We have tried to do so in many ways: by carefully observing nature, by studying its changes over time, by discovering similarities and differences, and by identifying the beings that surround us. We also used technology to make things easier, inventing more and more sophisticated tools.

As time went by, our relationship with the natural world began to change: we stopped being so afraid, and we no longer felt a need to communicate with nature or to thank it. Because nature became more or less under our control, we could use it to our advantage without worrying about the consequences.

After making a lot of mistakes, we learned that the planet has a limited capacity for renewal and also that everything on Earth is connected. If we destroy forests too quickly, they will end up disappearing completely. If we destroy the habitat of an animal, it will be in danger of extinction. If one species disappears, others will disappear. Everything works in a cycle, and we are a part of this cycle.

We try to deny it, but we are completely dependent on the planet and its resources. And, right now, nature is also dependent on us: we've become so powerful that we're capable of destroying a whole planet. And that's scary.

In spite of everything, we believe that humans have common sense. We didn't write this book out of panic that the planet would cease to exist; we wrote it with the conviction that the more we know, the better informed we are, and the more able we will be to appreciate and conserve the beauties and riches of the natural world.

Also, our experience tells us that contact with nature does us good. Spending time outside is relaxing and fun. It can make us more free and creative, more attentive and confident.

There are days when we feel like we don't have any energy, and other days when we feel like we have too much. In both cases, getting a bit of fresh air and getting close to nature can be all we need to feel better.

Nature . . . where are you?

Even if we live in the middle of the biggest city in the world, surrounded by big roads full of cars, there's always nature outside. The sky and stars (even if they're hidden by skyscrapers), clouds and rain, trees and flowers, and animals, lots of animals, are always there.

Animals? Where are the animals? (I never see them when I go out!)
Much of the time we're so distracted or in such a hurry that we don't even notice the small birds flying noisily above us, or the bats fluttering around a streetlight at dusk.

There are animals everywhere, but of course there are places where there are more of them and where they are easier to find. If you live in the country, you know this very well. All you have to do is walk away from the houses a little bit and you'll start to see different animals and plants.

In a city, there aren't so many different species, but they are still there . . . You just have to know where to look and, above all, you have to pay attention.

Yards and gardens are the easiest places to start, and most times you will find birds, small mammals, lizards, hundreds of insects, and other critters—on the ground, in the trees, or on plants.

If you want to see more species, or see a sky that will take your breath away, the best thing to do is go to the country: wherever you live, you can get to a forest, a river, or a mountain without traveling too far.

There's no limit to what we can learn outside. That might seem like an exaggeration, but it isn't. Every time we answer a question, many more arise. That's why the number of questions we can ask is infinite. In this book, we don't want to (and we wouldn't be able to!) answer all of them. We'll answer some, but many more will occur when you go outside.

Any plant you find, any tree you climb, any small creature you see has a story to tell and will make you ask lots of questions.

You might say, "But animals don't talk! And neither do plants!" Maybe not, at least not in a language we're able to understand right away, but this only makes the challenge more interesting.

Just like what happens when we hear a foreign language for the first time, we should also listen carefully to the language of nature. If we keep our senses alert, we'll be able to tell what plants, animals, stars, rocks, and everything else around us is saying.

In putting together this book, we paid particular attention to living things. That's our favorite topic and also the one that grabs the most attention when we go outside: the animals that pass by, the clues they leave, the trees that shelter them, and so on. But we've also tried to include other topics that anyone who leaves their house will encounter, like geology and astronomy.

Why did we decide to write this book?

It might seem that nothing is happening outside and that everything happens indoors: inside, we've got books, TV, computers, video games, movies . . .

But maybe that's not actually the case!

If you pay a little more attention—and this might be a different kind of attention than the one you use when you're watching TV or playing a computer game—you'll notice that *everything* is happening outside: the earth is spinning, clouds are moving, plants are sprouting up and dying, animals are busy going through their routines . . . We just have to make a little effort to learn to watch, and in the end, it can be much more rewarding than spending an afternoon on the sofa. (Of course, a screen can open up a whole world, but let's be clear: life on a screen is not the same as life in an anthill or a rock pool.)

We want this book to work as an incentive to leave the house. And we don't want it to become just a pretty display where you can see pictures of birds, clouds, or flowers. We want it to be a guide with ideas and practical information that will help you explore what you find outside.

There's a huge world waiting for you out there.
We hope you have lots of adventures!

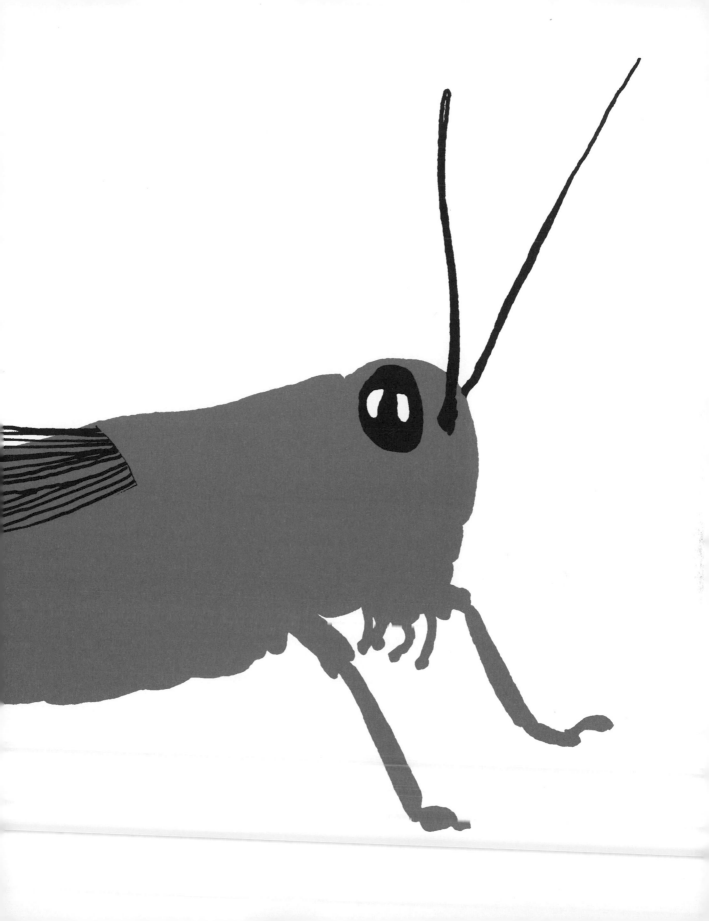

Where to go?

As we've already said, you can explore nature even in your backyard or the bit of land behind your house. In just trying to answer a simple question—how many different species of animals live here?—can provide a big enough challenge to keep you researching for a year. You might also just like to enjoy yourself without "scientific goals": try looking at the clouds, feeling the wind, climbing a tree, drawing flowers . . . You can do that almost anywhere!

Outside–inside cities

There are lots of species associated with urban areas. There are pigeons, sparrows, and sea gulls, of course, but if you pay a little more attention you'll likely see bats and birds of prey right in the city (like kestrels, which make their nests in tall buildings). These are just a few examples—and there are hundreds of others.

Outside–out of the cities

If you want to go on a bigger adventure, you can try to get to know a certain landscape or biotope. Outside of big cities we can find very different landscapes, some of which are very interesting from a natural point of view (especially when it comes to the variety of animals and plants).

Here are some of the most important places to explore:
Woods and forests

Forests and woods are always special places to visit, for their beauty, but also for the quantity and diversity of animals and plants that exist there. You'll certainly be able to see (and especially hear!) lots of birds singing and, if you're lucky, even hear a woodpecker "drumming" on a tree. If you look carefully, you'll see that tree trunks are covered with small insects, spiders and webs, mushrooms, lichens, and many other living things. Each tree is a forest and, in fact, a habitat in itself!

- - - - - - - - - - - - - - - -

If you are visiting a forest, wood or scrubland, check out the following chapters before you go: *The Things Animals Leave Behind; Bugs and Critters; Amphibians; Trees; Birds; Reptiles; Flowers,* and *Mammals.*

Most forests that we can visit have already been altered in some way by humans—for the production of wood or charcoal, for example. Some have even been planted on purpose to be commercially exploited. Native forests (i.e. with trees that exist naturally in the region) are generally richer in fauna and flora. The most common types of forest are conifer (such as pine forests) and broadleaf (such as oak forests).

Oak forests, for example, are native forests that used to cover a huge area. They mostly contain oaks, of course, but there can be other trees too, such as beech and birch. All these trees are deciduous (in other words, they lose their leaves in the coldest months). This is why oak forests change a lot with the rhythm of the seasons—what you'll find in spring will certainly be different to autumn. Notice how the dry leaves that have fallen to the forest floor can hide a lot of surprises! Old fallen trunks also deserve special attention—you'll no doubt see mushrooms and lots of critters.

- - - - - - - - - - - - - - - -

Relevant chapters if you are exploring a mountain: *The Things Animals Leave Behind; Bugs and Critters; Trees; Birds; Reptiles; Flowers; Mammals; Rocks; The Stars, the Moon, and the Sun* and *Clouds, Wind, and Rain.*

Mountains

Who's ever been up a mountain? It's definitely a unique feeling, getting to the very top! The landscape is often breathtaking, and, when we see the view for miles around, we can't help but think, "Yes! It was worth it!"

Climbing a mountain, or even just walking around the hills and valleys of a mountainous area, is almost always a guaranteed good day out. Lots of animals have adapted to live in these areas—birds are, as a general rule, the easiest to see (you'll likely see crows and birds of prey), but a closer look can reveal the odd mammal as well, and of course lots of flowers, if you go in spring. Keep an eye out for what you might find swimming in a mountain lake, too.

You'll notice that the highest parts of mountains don't usually have vegetation. This can be because the original forest has already been cut down, but in the highest mountains the most probable cause is the cold. As the altitude increases, the climatic conditions become harsher: the temperature gradually decreases, and the wind gets stronger. This is why few species are able to survive in the highest mountains.

- - - - - - - - - - - - - -

If you are visiting any of these sites, read these chapters first: *The Things Animals Leave Behind; Birds; Mammals; Oceans, Beaches, and Tide Pools,* and *The Stars the Moon, and the Sun.*

Beaches, oceans, and islands

Most of the time, when we go to the seaside in summer, we don't always remember that beaches are very rich in fauna (this is the place where sea and land meet, and so both species that live in the water or on land can be found here). On rocky beaches we can look for starfish, mussels, and crabs, and on sandy beaches you might find clams that live buried in the wet sand, and sandpipers that flit away from the waves as they hunt for the clams . . . And this is only what we see with our feet on dry land! With goggles and flippers we can discover a whole underwater world.

Islands are also very special places. Because they're surrounded by the sea, many of the animals that live there are unable to leave and so they evolve in isolation, giving rise to new species. This is why, on islands, there are usually lots of endemic species (species that don't exist anywhere else). This happens more frequently on remote islands, i.e. the ones that are furthest from the coast. On islands we can also find important colonies of marine birds.

- - - - - - - - - - - - - -

Most relevant chapters: *Bugs and Critters; Amphibians; Birds; Reptiles; Mammals; Oceans, Beaches, and Tide Pools,* and *Clouds, Wind, and Rain.*

Rivers, estuaries, and lakes

Wetlands such as rivers, estuaries, lakes, lagoons, and swamps, are some of the places where we can spot the most species of animals and plants. We'll see more birds than anything else (there can be thousands of them), but also lots of amphibians. With a bit of luck you might see a mammal, such as an otter or beaver. There are lots of fish, of course, but they're obviously not so easy to observe. Insects are also abundant—dragonflies, water striders and many more.

Arable land and pasture

Lots of animals are interested in the places we humans cultivate. This is because many of them like the food we grow—whether cereals, vegetables or fruits—and therefore they choose these places to feed or make their nests. Other animals simply like living underneath cultivated land, where they can dig their tunnels more easily—this is the case with moles.

- - - - - - - - - - - - - -

Before you go to a field, read the following chapters: *The Things Animals Leave Behind; Bugs and Critters; Amphibians; Trees; Birds; Reptiles; Flowers; Mammals; Rocks; The Stars the Moon, and the Sun*, and *Clouds, Wind, and Rain.*

Important things to know

Getting to know the natural world can be a fantastic experience, but there are certain things you should know to avoid dangerous situations.

Don't forget the following rules:

On trips to the country, you should always be accompanied by an adult or have their permission. And never go out alone. It will be safer; plus, if you've got company, you can always ask questions (or show them what you already know!).

Take advantage of nice days.
Sometimes you want to walk in the rain or feel the wind in your hair, but don't go outside in a storm, especially a thunderstorm. You can always admire the lightning from your window, inside your nice and cozy house.

Whether you're going to see the stars or amphibians, or hear owls singing, if you go out at night, remember that it's easy to get lost or trip on something. Always take a flashlight and a coat.

Pay attention to the path you take, especially when you're walking through a forest. It's very easy to get lost because you don't have points of reference and, suddenly, everything all around you looks the same. Take a compass if you have one; it might help you find the way back.

If you're going to explore near the sea, a lake, or a river, don't get too close to the water. There aren't crocodiles in many places . . . but a wave or a slippery stone could make you fall.

Also remember:

- Leave nests or burrows alone.
- Don't leave garbage on the ground or on riverbanks or in rivers.
- Don't pull up plants just for the sake of pulling them up.

- Avoid lifting stones. There might be animals using them as a hiding place.

- If you want to watch animals, try to stay silent so you don't scare them.

What to take with you

You certainly don't want to be cold, hungry, or uncomfortable when you go outside, so before you leave, make sure you have:

A hat and sunblock (Don't forget to apply sunblock regularly—in the countryside, you can get as much sun as you would during a day at the beach!)

A flashlight, in case you're out when it gets dark

Rain boots or shoes with rubber soles if you're going to watery places (such as rock pools)

Binoculars to see birds and other animals

A GPS or compass (Learn how to use them before you go!)

A notebook and pencil to write down and/or draw what you find

Comfortable boots (already broken in, of course)

A coat (Even if it's not chilly when you leave, the wind at the end of the day can become unpleasant.)

A flask, thermos, or bottle of water and a packed lunch

A guide to the countryside with helpful information, like names and details about animal and plant species, or types of rock—whichever are most appropriate for the places you're visiting. A guide to the stars would be great for a nighttime visit. You can take this book, too, of course!

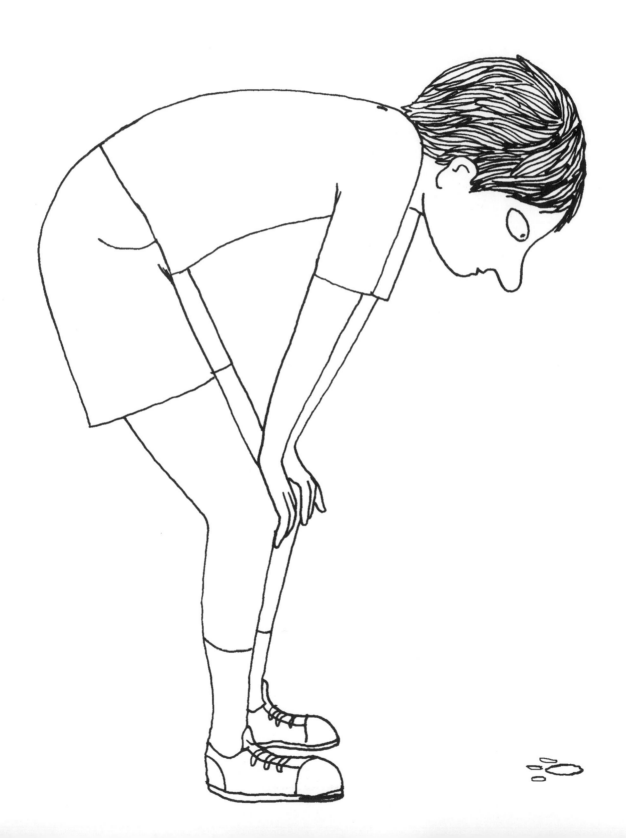

FOLLOW THE CLUES!

THE SIGNS ANIMALS LEAVE BEHIND

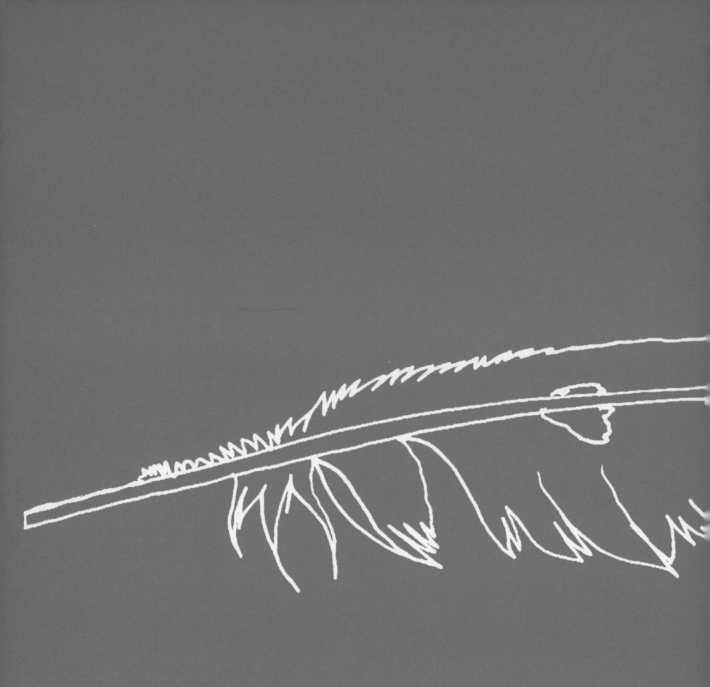

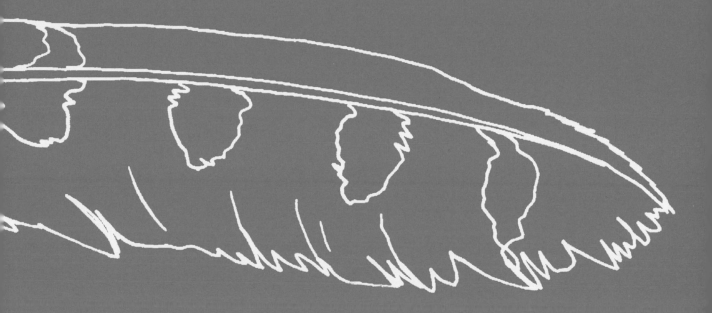

Everyone knows there are all sorts of creatures in the country, but how many of them have you actually seen? The truth is that many of them are hidden and are very hard to find. So how do people manage to study them and find out about their lives?

It's easy—you just have to follow the clues!

What kind of clues do animals leave?

Even though many people don't notice these clues, animals leave a lot of telltale signs behind. It's no wonder, because everything they do in their daily lives—eating, moving, sleeping, reproducing, or growing—leaves some sort of trace we can follow. Ready to investigate?

You are what you eat!

People leave aside bits of food they can't manage to eat, and animals do the same:

<u>Plant-eating animals</u> often leave behind chewed seeds, leaves, or fruits. All these leftovers help us find out exactly which animal was there. Even if there are other animals that eat the same foods, the way they eat is different. You just have to know the signs to look out for.

crossbill

For example, squirrels chew pinecones to get at the pine nuts. They strip off the scales and leave the core. The crossbill likes eating pinecones as well, but it opens them in a different way, so the leftovers look different: the edges of the scales appear ragged, whereas those stripped by a squirrel are cleaner.

<u>Meat-eating animals</u> also leave clues that let us know which has been doing the eating and which was eaten!

eagle

For example, many birds of prey eat other birds, leaving their plucked feathers behind. By looking at these feathers, we can find out which bird they belonged to.

Close-up clues

Pinecones and hazelnuts

If you find a chewed pinecone or hazelnut, try to figure out which animal it belonged to. Look at them carefully and compare them with these pictures.

This pinecone has been frayed and scratched by a woodpecker.

A squirrel has chewed this hazelnut and stripped this pinecone.

This pinecone and hazelnut have been chewed by a mouse.

A great tit has bored into this hazelnut.

Feathers

-- -- -- -- -- -- -- -- -- -- --

Types of feathers

When you find a feather, before trying to figure out which bird it belongs to, you can identify what kind of feather it is.

Flight feathers can be found on the wings and tail of a bird and are unmistakable because they're longer than other feathers and have a hard central shaft (rachis). Two types of flight feathers are shown here: the tail feathers are symmetric, while the wing feathers are asymmetrically shaped.

Contour feathers cover the rest of a bird's body. They also have a central shaft, but it's not as hard as the one in flight feathers. Contour feathers give the bird its smooth shape.

Down feathers are soft, fluffy feathers found underneath the other feathers. They don't have much of a central shaft, and their job is to keep the bird warm.

Which bird?

The shapes and markings of different feathers will help you figure out which birds they came from.

Owl feathers are very soft to the touch, especially the top part of the wing feathers.

With a bit of luck, you might also find **Jay feathers,** many of which have striped patterns.

If you live in a city, you will often come across **pigeon feathers,** which are normally small and white, black, or gray.

Better out than in!

Unlike the animals we've already talked about (which only eat what they can or what they like), there are others that swallow their prey whole and, after digestion, vomit the parts they're unable to digest. This is the case with the barn owl, which throws up small balls made from the bones and fur of the animals it eats.

Biologists call these balls pellets. They're great clues because they allow us to observe the regurgitated bones, which means we can perhaps figure out which animal they belonged to. With them, we can even assemble the complete skeleton of an animal that has been swallowed!

Animals and their (interesting) feces

Just like when humans eat, there are always parts of food the body rejects when animals eat, and these parts are sent out of the body as feces (the name biologists give to animal poop). In animal feces, we can find everything that wasn't digested, such as seeds, plants, fur, small bones, or insect exoskeletons.

The different shapes, sizes, "ingredients," and smells of feces can tell us what an animal ate, and we can also discover which animal produced it.

Walking, running, slithering

Have you noticed that when you walk barefoot on wet sand, you leave prints that are a perfect copy of your feet? If you rode a bike along the beach, what marks would you leave? Instead of prints, it would be a continuous track, like when you drag a stick along the ground.

The exact same thing happens with animals: the marks they leave on the ground can tell us what species they belong to, if it's an adult or a baby, and if the animal was running or walking.

Feet firmly on the ground

Animals have different legs and move in different ways. And, just like us, they can run, jump, hop, or simply walk. The number of legs each animal has can therefore give us lots of clues:

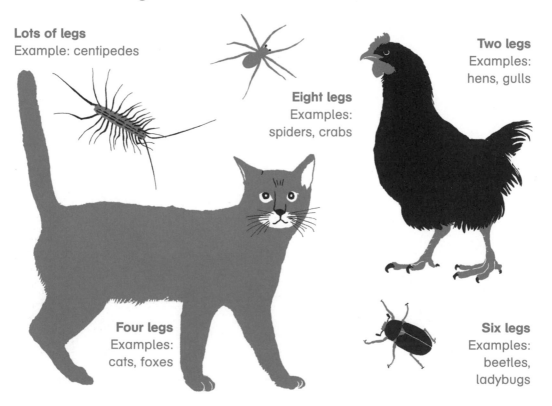

Lots of legs
Example: centipedes

Eight legs
Examples:
spiders, crabs

Two legs
Examples:
hens, gulls

Four legs
Examples:
cats, foxes

Six legs
Examples:
beetles,
ladybugs

Important footprints clues

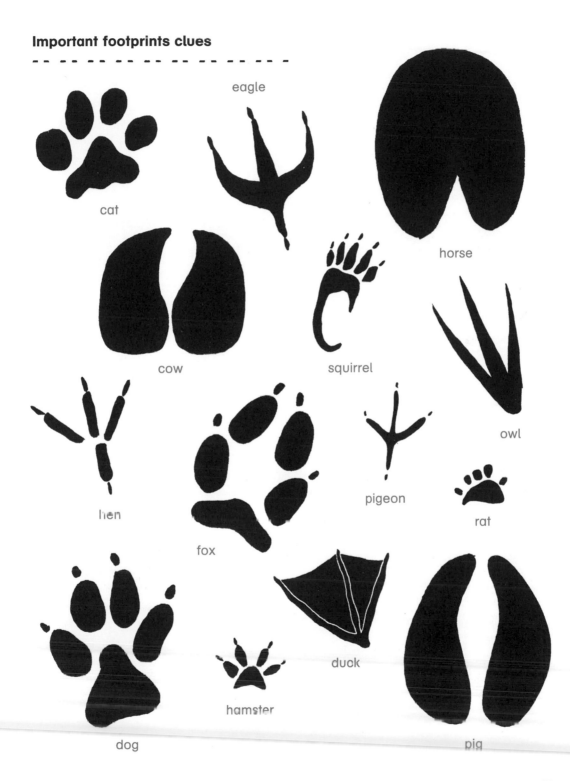

cat

eagle

horse

cow

squirrel

owl

hen

fox

pigeon

rat

dog

hamster

duck

pig

Slithering like a snake

Because they don't have legs, snakes leave very different tracks than other animals. When you find these marks, they are easy to identify.

Important snake track clues

- - -- - -- - -- -- -- -- - -- - -- - --

There are five main types of movement along the ground. Some of these movements are used more by certain species, but they can also vary with the condition of the ground: for example, if the ground is sandy or earthy, if the snake can move freely, or if there is little space around it.

1. Rectilinear: Made in open spaces by very big snakes, like the big constrictor species (e.g., anaconda).

2. Lateral slide: One of the most well-known tracks. Corresponds to tracks on sand and other slippery surfaces, such as those left by snakes in the desert.

3. Jumps:

4. Concertina: Often used to move through tight spaces, such as tunnels.

5. Lateral undulation: The most common among many species.

Always on the same path

There are animals that tend to take the same route somewhere (like you when you go to school each day). This means a path gets marked on the ground. If it's a big animal, a wide path is formed; if it's a small animal, a narrower path is formed.

Mammals are usually more difficult to see than birds, but fortunately they leave a lot of clues! Almost all of them leave tracks that we can identify:

- Just as their name suggests, water voles love water. To get there, they make a network of footpaths through the grass to better protect themselves from predators. These paths are about 4 in (10 cm) wide.
- Badgers (animals much larger than water voles) also leave paths in the places where they walk many times. These paths, which are about 12 in (30 cm) wide, lead to the entrances of their dens.

✳

Become an animal detective in the country!

- -

The edge of a river is an excellent place to see tracks because lots of animals go there to drink water, eat, or even take a dip!

Tips:

- To watch animals, you have to be cautious and silent, because otherwise your presence will scare them. Talk quietly, and communicate with your friends using gestures.

- Don't try to interfere with the animals you're watching. Don't give them food, don't try to "help them," and leave their nests or burrows alone.

❇

Become an animal detective in the city!

- -

Discover them all around!

Tips:

- You can take photographs or draw the footprints that you find. That way it's easier to study the shapes and spot the differences.

- Never touch animal excrement, because it might give you diseases. This is a job only for biologists, and must be done with the right equipment.

exuvias

Comfortable in your own skin!

Just like us, all other animals grow. There are some that never stop growing, even when they're really old, like octopuses, lobsters, or corals (they don't look like it, but corals are animals). Unlike our skin, some other animals' skins don't grow, which means their "owners" start to feel very squeezed inside it. That means it's time to undress!

Some examples

When animals "take off" their skin, they often leave it in the middle of the path, and that can be a great clue for us.

Among the animals that get "undressed" are snakes, which leave their old skin as if they're turning a sock inside out: they rub their bodies along the ground and vegetation until their skin comes off whole!

If you're lucky enough to find a snakeskin, you can try to see which part is the head. This is the part that lets you identify the snake down to its species.

There are other animals that change their skin, such as grasshoppers (in this case, it's not a "skin" but rather an exoskeleton, which is the name for a skeleton on the outside of the body). When they come out of the egg, grasshoppers are called nymphs and have a white exoskeleton. These nymphs grow, and at a certain size, they have to change the exoskeleton because they no longer fit inside it. That's why you can sometimes find these white exoskeletons (called exuvias) in the country or in a yard.

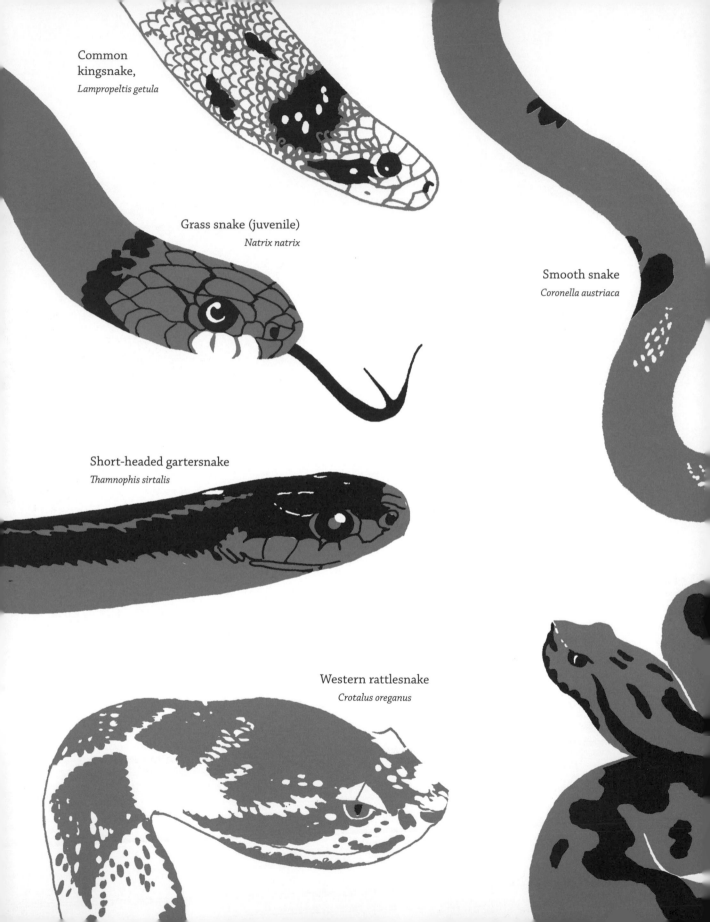

Common kingsnake,
Lampropeltis getula

Grass snake (juvenile)
Natrix natrix

Smooth snake
Coronella austriaca

Short-headed gartersnake
Thamnophis sirtalis

Western rattlesnake
Crotalus oreganus

Snakes are special because they shed their skins in one go, unlike other animals, whose skin comes off in pieces. You can tell if a snake is about to shed when its skin looks dull and its eyes go a cloudy blueish color.

Copperhead
Agkistrodon contortrix

Northern water snake
Nerodia sipedon

Adder
Vipera berus

Home, sweet home . . .

However much we like wandering around outside, there comes a time when we want to go home. Maybe because it's very cold, or it's going to rain, or we're tired and all we can think about is sleeping in our beds. The same happens with animals, or at least something similar.

Animals have houses different than ours (even if some live in our houses without us realizing) and their nests and burrows are also great clues.

Nests in the trees

There are lots of birds that make nests in the trees, like starlings—birds that are common almost everywhere and lay blue eggs. There are also mammals that make nests in trees, like dormice, which take advantage of openings and holes in trees to make their homes.

There are lots of different ways to make nests (you'll find more information on this topic in the "Birds" chapter).

Some prefer to have their houses underground

You might have already seen several heaps of soil close to one another in the country or in a yard. Have you ever thought what they might be?

To protect themselves, there are lots of animals that make burrows underneath the ground (and when they make these burrows, they leave soil outside, of course). These are excellent clues for us!

Now you know: holes in the ground or heaps of soil are a sign that somebody is down there making tunnels. These might be, for example, moles or voles.

There are clues to follow everywhere, so get going! You can look for clues on the beach, in the country, and even in the city.

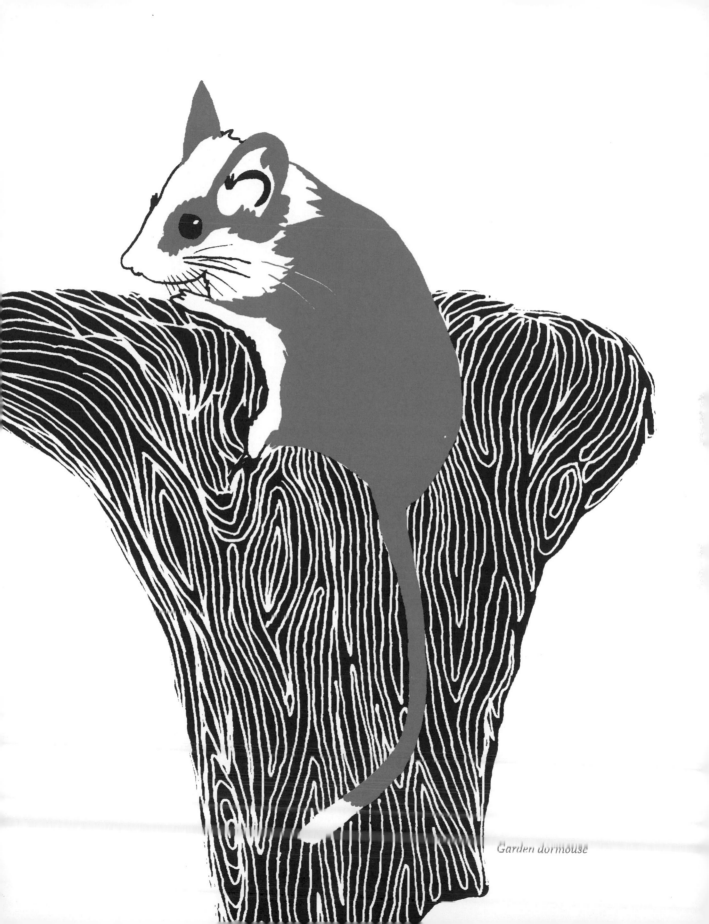

Garden dormouse

BUT WHAT KIND OF BUG CAN THIS BE?

BUGS AND CRITTERS

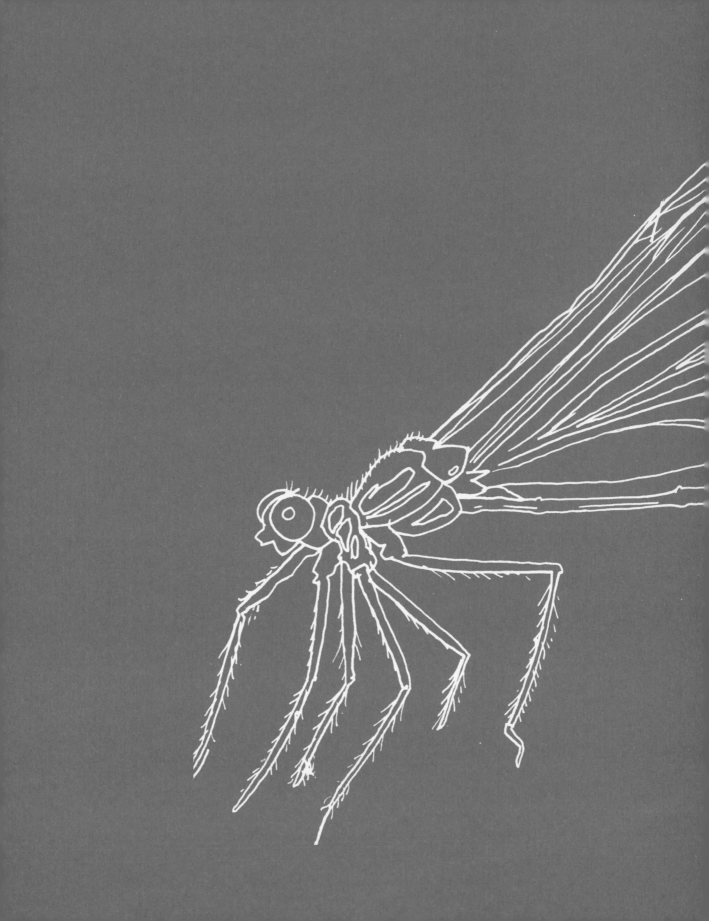

Not all animals are rare or hard to find. There are lots of bugs, creepy-crawlies, and critters that are very easy to spot and that we come across quite often, while they're climbing a wall, wandering across the ground in front of us, or fluttering around.

Worms, slugs, ants, butterflies, and snails: welcome to this book!

Let's start with worms . . .

All species of segmented worms have moist skin and a long, soft, tubelike body made of segments, or rings. It is these rings that give worms their special powers. What kind of powers, you ask?

When they lose one of their segments, these worms (like all annelids) can regrow it, an ability that is very useful. Imagine, for example, a robin pecks a worm: if the bird takes away a part of the worm's body, the worm is able to regenerate and survive.

Leeches and polychaetes are also annelids. Most leeches live in shallow freshwater and feed off the blood of other animals. Polychaetes are similar to worms, but they live in water. People often use them as bait for fishing.

Are there male and female worms?
No . . . and yes. Worms are hermaphrodites, which means they are male and female at the same time. Even though they have two sexes, a single worm cannot reproduce alone. It always has to find another worm, and after the two of them come together to reproduce, both can lay eggs.

Do worms have a heart?
Worms don't just have one heart—they have several! And some Australian species of worm are so long, growing up to 10 ft (3 m) in length, that they need 15 hearts to pump blood through their bodies.

The best way to learn about worms is by looking at them. Shall we?

● I caught a worm!

Worms like soil that's moist and not too hard, like the soil you find in most vegetable gardens. If you know somebody who has a vegetable garden, you can ask them if they often see worms (it's always a good idea to ask someone with experience). When you find a place with loose, moist soil, try digging a bit to look for worms. You can do this with a small spade or a trowel, or even with your hands. (If you don't want to get dirty, you can use gardening gloves.)

Tips:

● If the soil is very dry, wet it with a bit of water.

● Take a bucket and put a some soil inside it. You can put worms into the bucket for observation.

● Be careful when you dig so you don't cut any worms in half.

● Use the worms you collect to do the experiments we suggest on the following pages.

Look at worms through a magnifying glass

- - - - - - - - - - - - - - -

Place a worm on a piece of thick paper or cardstock. Wait for the worm to start moving across the paper.

Get close and try to hear the noise the setae make as the worm slides across the paper. Notice the way the worm's body contorts: that's the muscles contracting.

Run your hand over it slowly to feel the rings. If you've got a magnifying glass, you'll be able to better see all the details of its body.

- - - - - - - - - - - - - - -

How can worms move if they don't have legs?

On each of the segments of a worm's body, there are four pairs of tiny bristly hairs called setae. When worms move, they contort their muscles and the setae help, as if they were little legs.

Do the experiment on this page, and you'll be able to observe this.

Do worms have noses?

Worms don't have what we would usually call a nose, nor do they have lungs, because they use their skin to absorb the oxygen that is dissolved in damp soil. When it rains a lot and the soil gets full of water, there is no more oxygen and worms have to come to the surface to breathe.

Prove that worms have a special nose by doing the activity suggested on the right.

What do worms *do*?

It might not seem like it, but worms are very useful:

- Lots of animals eat worms, like robins, blackbirds, salamanders, badgers, and moles.
- Worms eat the remains of animals and plants and turn these remains into nutrients. These nutrients end up in the worms' poop (called castings), which is left behind in the soil, and then these nutrients can be used by plants. Worms are very important for fertilizing soil!
- Worms make a lot of tunnels, which let air and water into the soil, and this allows plants to get more nutrients.

Today there are factories where the workers are worms! What they do there is called vermicomposting. It's a strange name, but pretty simple: the worms turn organic waste (like food waste) into fertilizer for the soil.

Prove that worms have a special nose

- - - - - - - - - - - - - - - -

Put a worm on a damp cloth. Soak a cotton ball in acetone (ask an adult for help) and move it close to the worm's head, without touching the worm!

Now do the same at the other end of the worm and along its side. Notice how the worm reacts the same all over its body. This is because the worm smells the acetone in all its segments. In other words, its whole body is one big nose!

- - - - - - - - - - - - - - - -

Let's follow slugs and snails

How are slugs and snails related?
Both belong to a group called mollusks, the same group that includes octopuses, cuttlefish, squid, mussels, cowries, clams, and many others.

If they look so different, how can they all be mollusks?
Because they're all invertebrates, and they all have soft bodies without segments or rings. Many mollusks' bodies are divided into three parts: head, visceral mass, and foot (see illustration).

Why do snails carry their houses on their backs?
Snails hide inside their shells so they don't get eaten by predators. When it's hot out, the shell also protects their skin and prevents them from drying out and dying.

Just like our bones, snails' shells are made of calcium.

Visceral mass: The internal organs (e.g., heart and lungs) are found underneath the shell.

Foot: This is a very strong muscle and is the part that touches the ground.

Head: This is where the eyes and tentacles are found.

Why don't slugs have shells?

It's a well-kept secret, but most slugs do have shells—it's just that it's a small shell inside their body that lost its protective function thousands of years ago. No one knows exactly why slugs and other mollusks evolved to not have a shell or to have a reduced shell inside their body, but we think it was probably so they can explore other habitats better. Because a snail goes everywhere with its house on its back, it's certainly more difficult for it to get into tight places or go underneath logs or stones. Slugs, meanwhile, can easily slip through any crack, compressing their bodies and getting into places snails can't.

● **Look for snail shells**

Where: Near fences or stuck to posts.

○ Notice the different types and textures of shells (are they wrinkled or smooth?).

○ Organize them by size: younger snails have smaller shells (as the snail grows, the shell grows, too).

○ And finally, look which way the shells twist (left or right?). If all the spirals go the same way, then it's possible that they belong to the same species.

Geomalacus maculosus

●

**Look at bugs through
a magnifying glass**

- - - - - - - - - - - - - - - - - -

Bugs are almost always tiny
little things. With the help
of a magnifying glass, you
can get a better look at their
details: texture and colors,
eyes, legs, antennae, and
tentacles (if they have them).

Look carefully and draw all
the details you discover.

- - - - - - - - - - - - - - - - - -

Plagues or rare bugs?

Often, gardens are infested by a plague of snails,
with countless snails eating all the plants they
come across. However, there are species that
are in danger of extinction, despite how easily
they reproduce. This is the case with *Actinella
carinofausta*, a species unique to the island of
Madeira in Portugal.

The slug *Geomalacus maculosus* only lives in
Portugal, Spain, and Ireland and is protected
by conservation laws. When it feels threatened,
it rolls up completely into a ball-like shape, an
unusual characteristic in the world of slugs.

Do snails have teeth?

Snails mainly eat plants, but they can also eat
other snails and even bird poop! Slugs also eat
plants, mosses, and fungi, but some can be
carnivorous, eating other slugs, snails, worms,
and the remains of other animals.

Inside their mouths, both snails and slugs have
a radula, which looks like a grater made from
hard rubber. On the radula, there are rows and
rows of tiny teeth that break up food so it can be
swallowed.

Why do snails and slugs always leave slime?

We already know that snails and slugs are both mollusks, and they have something else in common: slime! They leave it wherever they go.

This slime is called mucus. Let's take a look at it and see what it does . . .

● Look at snail and slug slime

- -

When?
After it's rained. Slugs and snails like moisture.

Where?
You can find snails and slugs under logs and stones in a yard, garden, or open space.

Tips:

○ If you have a magnifying glass, take it with you.

○ Stay still while you wait and watch snails move. Notice how slowly they move and how they leave slime on the ground as they move. This slime helps them move on smooth surfaces, such as leaves, without slipping.

○ Slugs can produce two types of mucus (which can even be different colors): one that helps them move and another that protects their skin so it doesn't dry out.

○ If it's hot, try putting a snail on a smooth, dry surface, such as a cement floor. Notice how the mucus that the snail leaves on the ground doesn't make a continuous line, but leaves gaps. The snail is able to place its foot so it loses the least amount of mucus possible and therefore doesn't dehydrate.

Where are the eyes?

Slugs and snails have two pairs of tentacles on their heads. The eyes are on the upper tentacles, and the lower ones are used for smelling. Both are retractable, which means they can be pulled in. And if they're ever cut off, they can grow right back.

Do you believe in Cupid?

You might not, but he exists . . . in the form of a snail.

When a snail wants to mate with another snail, it gets up close and pricks it with a kind of dart. This dart contains substances that increase the chances of fertilizing the chosen snail—it is called a gypsobelum, or a love dart.

Just like worms, slugs and snails are hermaphrodites. When two of them reproduce, both can lay eggs: they make a hole in the ground and lay the eggs there, normally several dozen eggs. When they hatch, the snails are already wearing their shells!

● **How many legs?**

Whenever you see a bug, count how many legs it has. Beetles, like this one here, have three legs on each side of their body.

If you find a creepy-crawly with six legs, you know that it's an insect. Ladybugs, grasshoppers, ants, and cockroaches all have six legs. But even though they have the same number of legs, one insect's legs can be very different than the legs of another. (See the opposite page for some different kinds of legs.)

Different kinds of legs

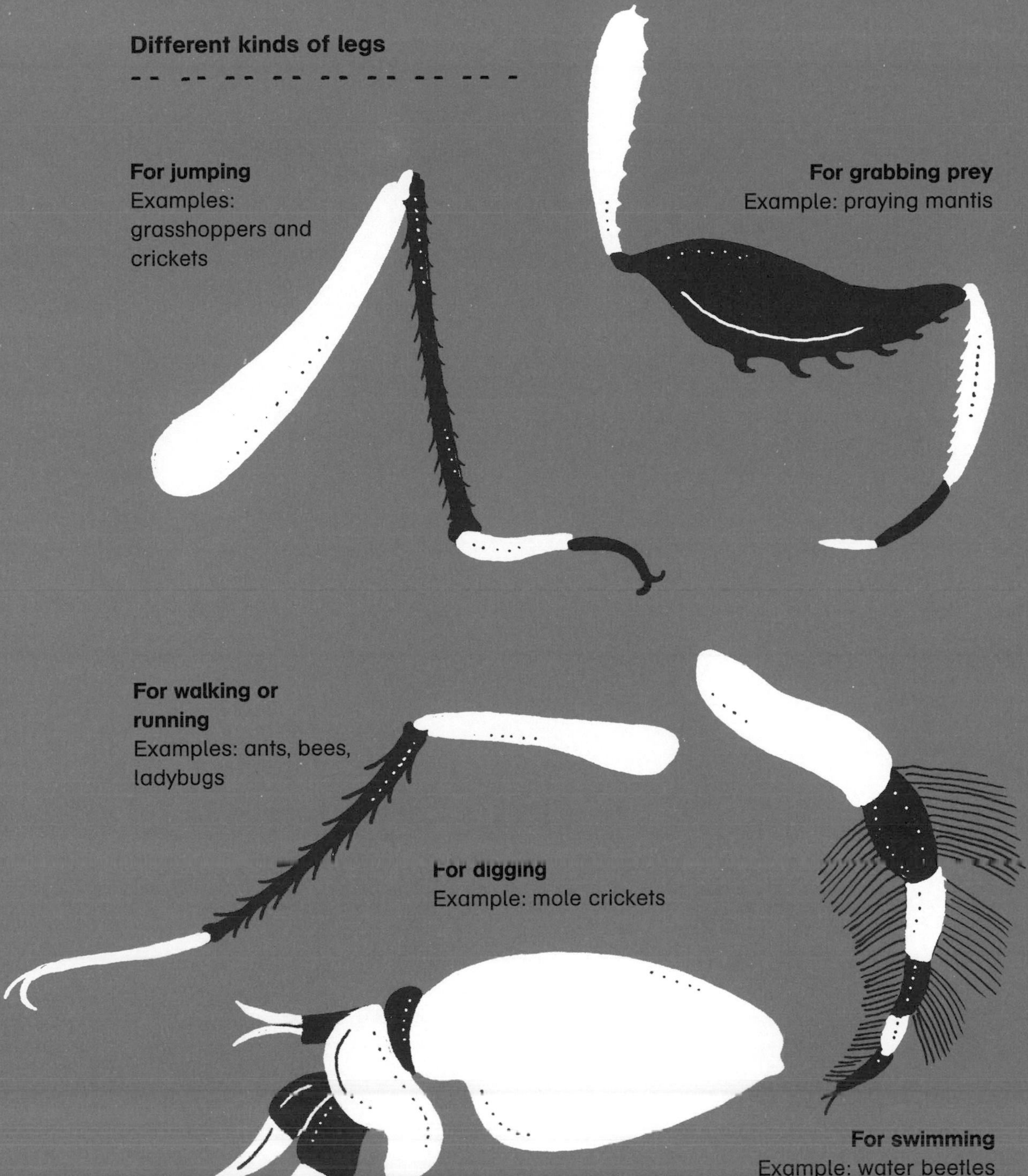

- - -- -- -- -- -- -- -- -

For jumping
Examples:
grasshoppers and
crickets

For grabbing prey
Example: praying mantis

**For walking or
running**
Examples: ants, bees,
ladybugs

For digging
Example: mole crickets

For swimming
Example: water beetles

Go out at night and watch fireflies

Fireflies like dark places because they communicate using a language made of glowing lights. (And if there's a lot of light out, the other fireflies can't see the messages they're trying to send.)

Where to look?
You are most likely to find fireflies in areas with a lot of natural vegetation. (However, you can also find fireflies in a yard or garden.)

Look for them in the most hidden (and the darkest) places, in vegetation close to the ground.

When?
Fireflies can only be seen at the end of spring and in the summer. But still, sometimes it's not too easy to find them.

You know what to do—look for them in the dark!

An interesting fact: Did you know that the eggs of some species of fireflies are also luminous?

Ants and other insects

Insects are one of the most abundant groups of animals on our planet.

There are so many insects around the world that scientists can't decide how many species there are in total. (Some say there are 5 million; others think there are 100 million). So far, we know of almost one million species, but who knows how many more there are.

Unlike some animals we've already discussed, insects are tougher because they have a covering on the outside of their bodies. Because it's hard and outside the body's muscles, this covering is called an exoskeleton, which means a skeleton on the outside of the body.

Because there are so many of them and because they are all around us, insects are some of the easiest animals to find.
Shall we take a look?

●

Little ant, where are you?

- -

Go out onto the sidewalk searching for ants. Look for them on the trunks of trees, on plants, or in the soil. Because they're so small, you'll have to pay close attention.

When you find an ant, look at it closely. All ants are smooth and normally dark-colored: black, brown, or dark red. Unlike worms or snails, which have soft and sticky-looking skin, ants have harder bodies. Now you know it's their exoskeletons that make them look like that.

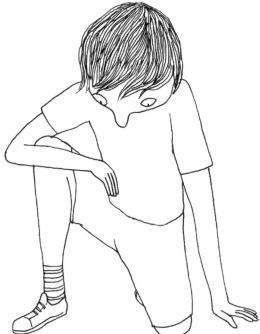

Why do ants touch each other with their antennae?

Ants' antennae are articulated, which means that they're made up of several pieces joined together. The main function of the ants' antennae is to pick up smells. Every ant has two antennae, which helps them determine the direction a smell is coming from.

When two ants meet, they touch antennae to pick up the other's scents, and this is how they communicate. For example, if an ant is hungry, it tells the other one by giving off a certain smell. This smell can even "ask" the other other ant to regurgitate food for it to eat. It may seem like a strange snack, but not for an ant.

Lots of other insects have antennae, and normally the main function is the same: to smell. There are species, like certain moths, that have such big antennae that they're able to pick up smells from miles away!

Feed an anthill

Spread little pieces of bread, cookies, or fruit (cut up very small) in the area around the anthill. Sit back and watch the ants have a feast!
Be careful: Don't leave food inside the anthill or block the entrance!

Draw a map of the anthill

Follow the ants when they come out of the anthill, marking the route they take. Plot the paths around the anthill, including the biggest obstacles for the ants (normally the path takes a detour and doesn't go over them) as well as any other obstacles you come across

What's life like in an anthill?

Ants live in a very organized society, which means that each type of ant has a different job in the anthill.

Living in an anthill, you will usually find:
- a <u>queen</u> **(1)**, which is normally bigger than the other ants and lays eggs constantly throughout her life;
- the <u>workers</u> **(2)**, which are females responsible for maintaining and defending the anthill;
- in some anthills, <u>soldiers</u> **(3)**, which are bigger and stronger and defend the anthill from invaders;
- the <u>males</u> **(4)**, which have a reproductive role.

An anthill is divided into various chambers, which are sort of like rooms. In the <u>pantry</u> **(5)**, the ants store seeds and other food, such as decomposing leaves. Do you know why? Because on these leaves, some species of ant grow fungi that they eat.

In the <u>nursery</u> **(6)**, the workers look after the larvae that will become baby ants. In the <u>storeroom</u> **(7)**, which is found at the bottom of the anthill, the ants store garbage (e.g., remains of leaves and dead ants); they care a lot about hygiene. In an anthill, there can also be <u>traps</u> **(8)**, false tunnels to make potential invaders waste time if they attack the anthill.

Why do some ants have wings?

Only the reproductive ants (female and male) are born with wings, and at a certain stage, thousands of them fly out of the anthill for their nuptial flight, to reproduce and to form new anthills. After copulation, they lose their wings. Then the females become new queens and the males die. The wings are only used by the ants to move to new places, far away from their anthill, and start everything again!

●

Look for different types of ants

- - - - - - - - - - - - - -

It'll be difficult to see the queen because she's very well protected inside the anthill. But you can try and find soldier ants and worker ants. You'll see that the soldiers have bigger heads and mouthparts and stay close to the entrance of the anthill.

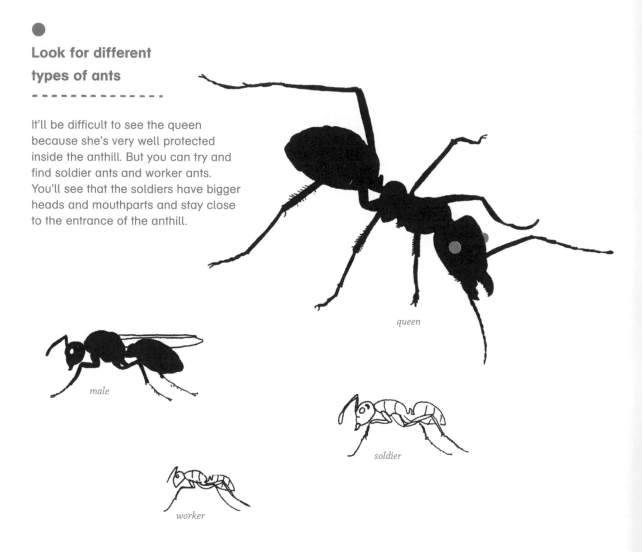

queen

male

soldier

worker

Is it true that in summer while the ants work, the cicadas sing?
It is technically true that ants spend the summer working, while the cicadas sing, but this doesn't mean that one is hardworking and the other's lazy! Only adult male cicadas sing, to attract females. If the females like the song, they come close so they can reproduce. (Everything in nature has a function!)

Some cicadas sing so loudly that they're able to wake us up at night, and there are some species whose song is so sharp that, even though it's not perceptible to the human ear, it can make some dogs howl in pain! Cicadas even have to protect themselves from their own singing: both males and females have eardrums shaped in a way that the sound doesn't cause internal damage.

If you try to capture a cicada and it flies away, you'll see that it leaves a liquid behind. It's not urine—it's just water or sap. Some biologists think that when cicadas flee, they get rid of some weight to make themselves lighter and more agile.

● **Use colors to attract insects**

You can try this trick to attract insects:

Put colored plates (yellow, blue, red) in the sun, with a few drops of water in them. Then sit down and watch the insects that arrive, attracted by the colors and by the water.

Where?
In a garden, yard, or in the country.

When?
Choose a sunny spring day.

cicada

81

Why do ants almost never leave the path?

Ants communicate with one another using chemical substances called pheromones. For example, when an ant finds food, it has to take it to the anthill and also tell the other ants about the location of the food so they can go and bring back the rest of it. The ant leaves pheromones along the way so that the others can follow. As more and more ants go to that place, more pheromones are left. The more ants that go there, the stronger the smell becomes and the more ants it will attract. Do you know why ants all walk in single file? It's because they're following each other's smell.

Intruders

As we've already seen, ants have everything they need inside the anthill: a nursery for the larvae, pantries with food, the queen's room, and even, just imagine, a trash can.

Write a diary of the life of an ant

- - - - - - - - - - - - - - - -

Sit next to an anthill and watch what happens: ants and their "deliveries" going in and out, as well as what goes on all around the anthill. You can watch the anthill and the ants for a few minutes or throughout a whole week, and note down the changes. (Imagine if it rains—what would happen?)

Look at the ants' paths

- - - - - - - - - - - - - - - -

Find an anthill or an ant's path. Look at the way the ants walk; they hardly ever leave the path. Also notice how the ants touch each other's antennae when they pass each other. Try an experiment, and put a piece of food that ants like (they prefer sweet things) just off the path. Now wait to see what happens . . . Will the ants find their way to your treat?

Anthills are warm and cozy in the winter and cool and airy in the summer. Because anthills are so comfortable, other insects want to live there. And sometimes they do.

Some of these intruders are <u>broad-headed bugs</u> **(1)**, <u>beetles</u> **(2)**, <u>flies</u> **(3)**, <u>moths</u> **(4)**, and <u>spiders</u> **(5)**. These animals disguise themselves using the scent of ants so the ants won't attack them. And where do they get this scent?

Most intruders in anthills can naturally imitate the smells and behavior of ants. Other species can extract chemical substances from the wax that covers the bodies of dead ants, and then spread it over their own bodies. This way, when an ant walks past them, the ant doesn't even notice that these insects don't belong in the anthill.

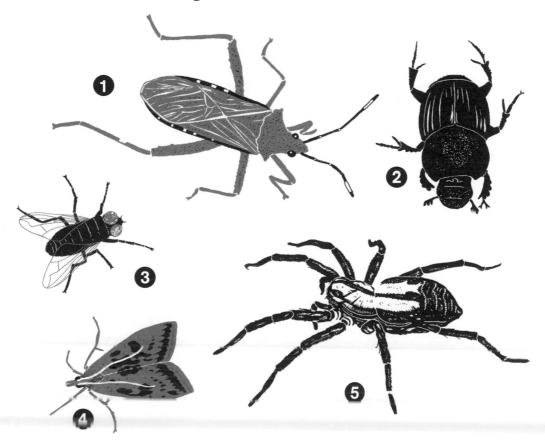

Butterflies

If you manage to get close enough to a butterfly to count its legs, you'll see that there are six, as with all insects. You'll also be able to appreciate its amazing body.

Butterflies with large wings (1) can glide long distances without flapping very often. Those with smaller wings have to beat them faster—some up to 80 times per second.

A butterfly's eyes (2) are made up of thousands of tiny lenses. Still, butterflies can't see very clearly and are unable to detect slow movements.

Some species of butterfly have "ears" (3) at the base of their wings, which allow them to hear birds or other hunters. A butterfly's feelers, or antennae (4), work like a nose to help it find food. They stick out from its body so it can sense which direction different smells are coming from. They also help the butterfly balance.

The mouth is a tube called a proboscis. It works like a straw, allowing the butterfly to suck up nectar from flowers. When the butterfly is resting, the proboscis stays rolled up, but it when it drinks it unfurls . . . sluuurp!

And how does a butterfly get its incredible colors? From the pigments of the plants that it ate when it was just a caterpillar.

How is a butterfly born?

-- -- -- -- -- -- --

Butterflies lay eggs. From an egg comes a caterpillar that eats a lot, growing bigger and bigger. Then it sheds its skin to reveal a case underneath called a chrysalis, or pupa. Inside the chrysalis, the caterpillar changes, and a brand-new butterfly emerges! This kind of transformation is called a metamorphosis.

Go out to look at butterflies

When?
The best time of year for observing butterflies is between March and September, because these are the months when there are more flowers and more sunlight—butterflies' favorite things! Choose a day when it isn't windy, since butterflies are sensitive insects. The best time of day is between 11 a.m. and 4 p.m.

Where?
Try walking anywhere that there are flowers, and look carefully.

What to do?
When you see a butterfly, first write down what color it is. At the end of your observation, you'll have the number of each color of butterfly. Then, later, you can investigate which species are the colors you saw more of, and you might come to some conclusions.

To help you, look for the butterfly species page in the center of the book.

IS IT A FROG

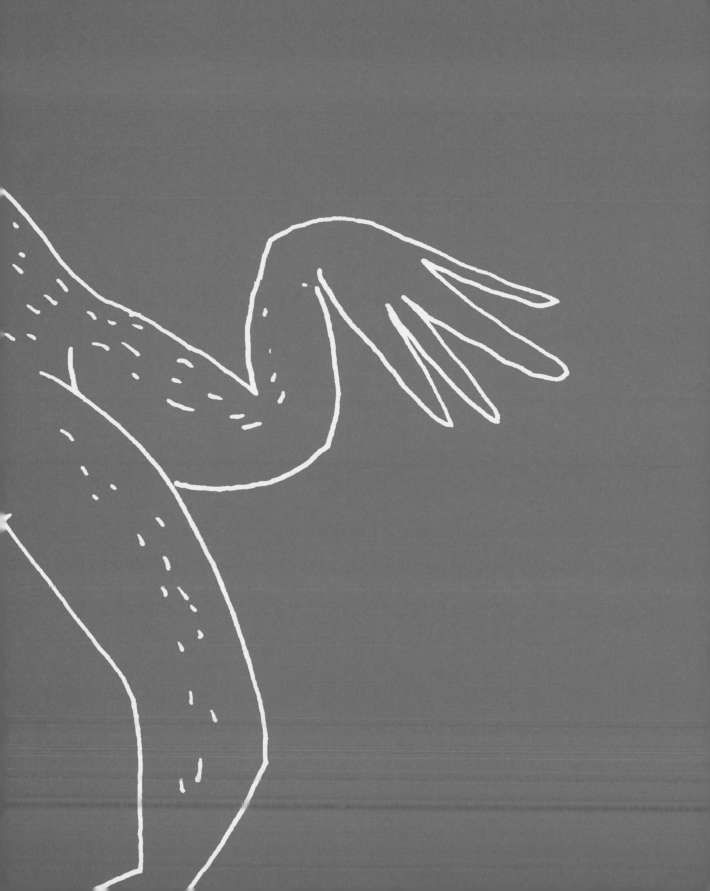

Do you hear that?
Those're toads, right?
(Or are they frogs?)
Do toads make noise on summer nights?
Do they try to outsing one another?
Do they sing their tadpoles to sleep?

Shall we go outside to see if we can hear them?

Amphibian? What kind of animal is that?

The word amphibian comes from the ancient Greek *amphibios*, which means "two lives." But do amphibians really have two lives? Maybe . . . When they're really small, frogs and toads are tadpoles, and they live in the water, where they breathe through gills like fish. But when they grow, they lose their tails, their gills become lungs, and they go live on land. It's like they do actually have two lives: one in the water and another on land.

Do you want to get to know them better?
A frogs' <u>skin</u> is smooth, without fur or scales. It is also thin and permeable to let water and oxygen through, because frogs mainly breathe through their skin. (Their lungs are very simple and not very efficient.)

Most frogs come out of their hiding places at night, when the temperature is lower and there is no danger of getting exposed to the sun. That way, their skin doesn't dry out so easily!

Did you know that frogs shed their skin like snakes? When the skin gets old, they pull it off with their feet, and sometimes they even eat it.

Frogs' <u>nostrils and eyes</u> are found on the top of their heads, which allows them to keep their bodies in the water, but their eyes and nostrils out.

Frogs and toads have almost always very small teeth and a lot of them don't have teeth at all, but their <u>jaws</u> are strong and help them swallow their food.

Some species are able to stick their <u>tongues</u> out to grab food.

Frogs don't have ears, but they do have <u>eardrums</u> on the outside of their heads. (Look for the round patches in the area behind the eyes.) They have excellent hearing!

Male frogs croak, or make sounds, to attract females during mating season. To croak, they fill their <u>vocal sacs</u> (the "pouches" under their chins) with air.

Some species are able to jump 20 times farther than their own length. This is because they have special <u>legs</u>: their back legs are much longer than their front legs, which helps them get their balance when jumping. It also makes them look like they're always sitting down.

fire salamander

Why are there such colorful amphibians?

Some amphibians are colorful to attract attention. The colors are used to warn predators: "These colors mean I'm not at all tasty—I'm even sort of toxic!"

Fire salamanders, which are all black with yellow spots (sometimes red), release toxic substances from their parotid glands (the raised parts on their heads behind their eyes). A snake would eat a salamander and vomit it right back up . . . it made him feel sick!

Some substances released by amphibians are not poisonous, but they can irritate our eyes. That's why you should always wash your hands after you touch an amphibian.

Where do these toxic substances come from?

Almost all of them originate from the insects that amphibians eat.

Curious amphibians

- - - - - - - - - - - - - - -

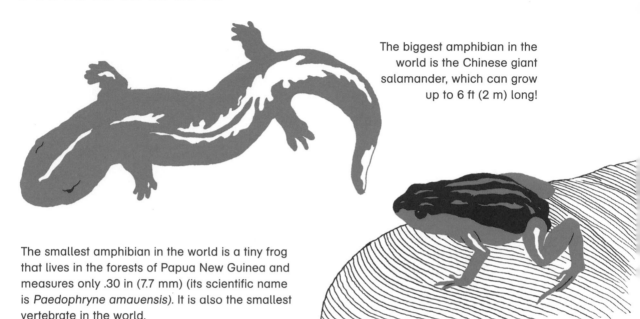

The biggest amphibian in the world is the Chinese giant salamander, which can grow up to 6 ft (2 m) long!

The smallest amphibian in the world is a tiny frog that lives in the forests of Papua New Guinea and measures only .30 in (7.7 mm) (its scientific name is *Paedophryne amauensis*). It is also the smallest vertebrate in the world.

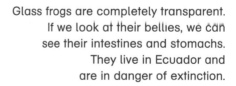

The genus name for midwife toads, *Alytes*, comes from the Latin *Allium*, which means "garlic." That's because when they're disturbed, they leave a strong smell of garlic.

Glass frogs are completely transparent. If we look at their bellies, we can see their intestines and stomachs. They live in Ecuador and are in danger of extinction.

Reinette apples got their name because their peel looks like toad skin (reinette comes from the Latin word *rana*, meaning "frog").

One of the strongest poisons in the world comes from a small frog in the Amazon rainforest, and it is used by indigenous people for hunting. For a guaranteed result, it's enough for them to simply touch the tips of their arrows on this frog's back.

But if they taste so bad . . .

What would want to eat them?

Even though they taste "bad," amphibians have lots of predators:

- Water snakes (1) eat toads (2) and frogs (3) when they're still tadpoles (4);
- Freshwater fish (5) also eat lots of amphibian larvae (6) (and can even cause their extinction in some places);
- other animals like storks (7), barn owls (8), and polecats (9) also like to eat amphibians.

And do you know what else? Other amphibians! One fire salamander will eat another fire salamander! Yikes!

And speaking of food . . .

-- -- -- -- -- --

Do you know what amphibians eat?

Amphibians are mainly carnivores, which means they eat other animals: spiders, worms, insects, etc. But when they're still larvae (tadpoles), frogs and toads are mainly herbivores.

-- -- -- -- -- --

All amphibians, but different

In many places around the world, there are only two types of amphibians: anura and urodela.

In some tropical countries, there is a third type called apoda (amphibians that don't have a tail or legs and look a bit like worms).

How to tell anura and urodela apart

- -

Anura don't have tails. Their back legs are bigger than their front legs, so they have to stay doubled up, which means that these animals look like they're always sitting down. Examples: toads, frogs, and tree frogs.

tree frog

Urodela have tails. Their front and back legs are almost the same size. Examples: salamanders and newts.

salamander

marbled newt

Some dance and others sing, but all for romance!

When it comes to finding a partner to mate with, amphibians are different: frogs and toads prefer to sing, while newts and salamanders prefer to dance a few steps.

Every species of toad or frog has a special song to attract a mate. Following lots of rain on spring and autumn nights, we can often hear males singing in the hope of attracting a female.

In the dances of salamanders and newts, males chase the females and dance in front of them with repetitive movements.

Salamanders do their dance on land. All other species of urodela do their dance in water, which makes it more difficult for us to see.

In many species, the males become better looking during mating season: they can become more colorful or develop crests on their backs, like marbled newts do.

❖
Catch frogs

- - - - - - - - - - - - - - - - -

During spring and summer, you can use a net to try to catch frogs from a nearby marsh or riverbank.

You might catch frogs as well as newts, tadpoles, salamanders, and small water insects.

Remember to return them to nature after you've observed them.

Don't forget:
Frogs are cold-blooded animals, which means that some species have to hibernate in winter to survive. Some also hibernate in summer (which is known as estivation)

- - - - - - - - - - - - - - - - -

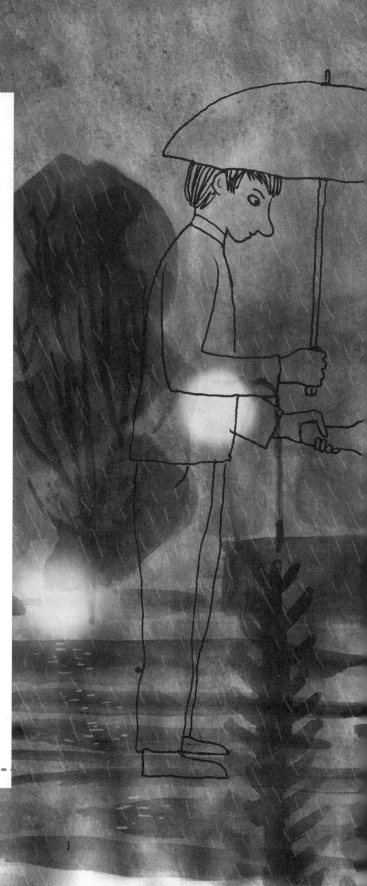

♣

Go on a nocturnal outing to hear amphibians sing

Some amphibians sing to call to their partners! (The purpose of this is to court or mate with them.)

Organize an outing to hear and observe them.

When?
At night, of course!

The best time of year is in January to March, because this is when it rains a lot and amphibians reproduce.

Where?
Wetlands, such as ponds and marshes, are best.

Tips:
- Go out after it's rained a lot. This is when amphibians like frogs and toads are most active.
- Wear rain boots or other waterproof boots.
- Because it'll be nighttime, take a coat and a flashlight. Be careful and look where you put your feet! Always make sure you go with an adult.
- Use a handheld recorder to capture the sounds of amphibians. Later, you can play the sounds in other places where you're looking for amphibians, and you can see if you get an answer. You can also find CDs with identified recordings of various species.

It's not just hens that lay eggs

Almost all amphibians lay eggs as well.

Most frogs, toads, salamanders, and newts are oviparous: they lay eggs, and their young grow inside these eggs until they're ready to come out. Frogs and toads lay eggs in groups; salamanders and newts lay single eggs.

Less common are amphibians that are ovoviviparous, like the fire salamander. This means the egg develops inside the mother's body.

It's possible to identify amphibians from the eggs they lay

- - - - - - - - - - - - - -

Common parsley frog
It lays dark eggs, wrapped in a transparent gelatinous film, forming very wide, short strands.

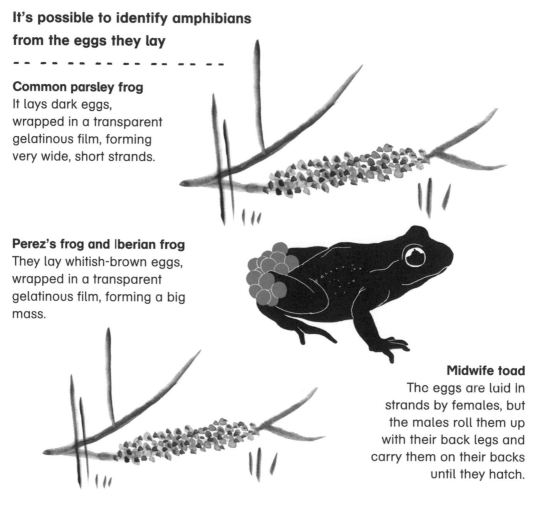

Perez's frog and Iberian frog
They lay whitish-brown eggs, wrapped in a transparent gelatinous film, forming a big mass.

Midwife toad
The eggs are laid in strands by females, but the males roll them up with their back legs and carry them on their backs until they hatch.

The mystery of the disappearing frogs

A few years ago, scientists noticed that various species of amphibians were at the point of extinction all over the world. We don't know exactly what's causing this decline (which is the name for this type of large-scale extinction), but we think it could be several things happening at the same time:

- One of the reasons may be the destruction of habitats. Without places to live and find food, amphibians can't survive.
- Another reason may be the appearance of new predators (animals that eat amphibians and previously didn't exist in their habitats), a phenomenon that often happens because humans take species to places where they didn't exist before (called the introduction of exotic species). For example, the Louisiana crawfish (which comes from the United States) was introduced to rivers in Europe. This crawfish eats the larvae of many European species, and since the "European" amphibians aren't familiar with the crawfish, they don't flee and are easily caught.
- Other reasons include diseases caused by fungi and viruses, an increase in toxic substances in the environment, climate change, etc.

And why do amphibians suffer more from these problems than other animals in the wild?

Because their skin is very permeable, which means it lets substances through. When water gets polluted, it's easy for dangerous substances to pass through amphibians' skins and get into their bodies. The same thing happens with toxins or fungi that are in the air or on the soil. Biologists discovered all this when studying animals at risk of extinction. One of the first species they investigated was the golden toad (*Incilius periglenes*), which lived in Costa Rica and is now extinct.

Frog or toad?

It is not so easy to tell the difference between frogs and toads at first sight. Normally people call frogs the animals with smoother skin that live close to water, and they call toads the ones with rougher skin that spend more time on land. But in fact, frogs and toads are related, and scientists don't think there's any real difference between them.

Tree frogs are easier to identify because they have a kind of suckers on their feet, which makes them such good climbers.

Some unique species

- - -- -- -- -- -- --

The **Iberian spadefoot toad** got its name because it has a kind of black spade (a callus) on its back legs. It helps it bury itself in sand to escape from predators and to hide from the sun and survive in the dry season.

The **fire salamander** got its name because people say it hatches in the flames of fire. This story must have come about because these animals sometimes hide in firewood and so when people were about to light the fire, salamanders would start to come out. After all, no one likes to be roasted— not even a salamander!

- - -- - -- - -- - --

toad

tree frog

Would you like to kiss a frog to see what happens? You shouldn't! Instead of bringing you a prince, kissing one will probably just make you itch.

Victors and victims

We know of almost 7,400 species of amphibians across the whole world. Some have adapted themselves to very particular habitats and even a small change could be enough to make them extinct. There are other species that aren't so specialized, which means they're able to live in very different habitats, distributing themselves in various countries or even whole continents. And when one of these more adaptable species is taken by humans to another region, the consequences are almost always bad.

A common amphibian victor

<u>African clawed frog</u>

The African clawed frog is a good example of a species that went far beyond its original area of distribution. It is native to the rivers and lakes of southeast Africa, but today the species is found throughout various parts of Europe, North America, South America, and Asia.

How did it all begin? The African clawed frog has often been chosen by scientists for laboratory experiments, such as the pregnancy test. In the past, women had to go to the doctor to find out if they were pregnant. A bit of their urine would be injected into a frog and if the woman was pregnant, the next morning there would be eggs in the aquarium! (Who knows how they discovered this!) It is thought that a lot of these animals were released into the wild when pregnancy tests stopped being done in this way. And that was when everything got messy.

These frogs are voracious and eat almost everything they come across—including the tadpoles of other amphibians. They also spread disease, and hence upset the balance of ecosystems around the world.

Some species that are victims

Red-backed salamander

While some amphibians have spread like a plague, others are suffering the consequences of the arrival of new species in their habitats. The Quito stubfoot toad and the Las Vegas Leopard frog are examples of amphibians that became extinct as a result of exotic species. The trout was responsible for the Quito stubfoot toad's disappearance, and in the case of the Las Vegas Leopard frog it was the bullfrog's fault. Even very abundant species can suffer the consequences of the introduction of exotics. This is the case of the red-backed salamander, a common species in various North American states. This long, thin salamander lives on land and likes hiding under tree trunks, moss and fallen leaves, in various kinds of forest. When there began to be exotic worms in some areas of the United States, it was verified that the number of salamanders decreased a lot. The worms reduce the amount of dead leaves on the forest floor, lowering the number of small animals that like this habitat and provide food for red-backed salamanders.

The salamander's trick

- - -- - -- - -- - --

The red-backed salamander is also an endangered species, and it has a unique ability: unlike most other amphibians, it can shed its tail to distract predators. While the predator is busy eating its tail, the salamander can run away! This ability to voluntarily cast off a body part, and still live, is called **autotomy**.

- - -- - -- - -- - --

LET`S SIT IN THE SHADE

TREES

Lying under a tree on a hot day, we may just want to keep perfectly still, appreciating the peace and quiet of the shade.

If we look and listen carefully, though, we'll quickly discover that we're not alone: trees are the home and feeding place of lots of animals and sometimes a real playground where they hide, run, and climb.

You might get up from the shade and think, *Why don't I climb this tree, too?*

Branches: The branches support the leaves and flowers.

Crown: The crown, or the top part of the tree, is made up of branches and is where the leaves, flowers, and fruit are found.

Trunk: The trunk is the woody part that supports the weight of the tree.

Roots: The roots fix the tree to the ground. Roots work like a straw: the tree sucks food and water from the soil through them.

What is a tree?

A tree is a living being and belongs to the plant kingdom.

A tree has roots, a trunk, and a crown.

Compared to other plants, a tree can be very big!

And how does a tree grow so tall without falling down?

Trees have roots that grab on to the soil, and also a very strong trunk, which is able to support the weight of all the branches and leaves. (If the tree didn't have these, it would spread out low on the ground, like many other plants.)

What is the difference between a tree and a shrub?

A tree has a main stem (or trunk) and a crown with lots of branches, while in general, a shrub has several stems that grow from the ground. Normally, experts say that an adult tree is one that reaches at least 10 ft (3 m) in height.

- -

Speaking of height, did you know that the tallest tree in the world is a coast redwood, which can grow to be 380 ft (115 m) tall? That's the same as a 38-story building!

As well as being very tall, sequoias are considered to be the oldest living beings on the planet; some are more than 4,000 years old.

- -

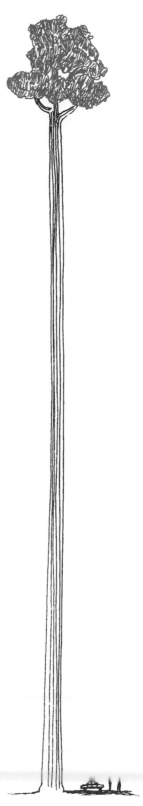

How do they grow?

Trees can grow in two ways: upward (in height) and outward (in width). This growth is accomplished by very active cells called meristematic cells. These cells are always multiplying and are able to make every kind of cell the tree needs: cells to make bark, flowers, and fruits.

What is there inside a trunk?
In a tree trunk, there is a very thin layer of cells called the cambium (2). The cambium is a factory that produces wood in two directions: inward, forming a layer called the xylem (1); and outward, building the phloem and the bark or the suber (cork tissue) (4).

With each year that goes by, the cambium makes new layers of these cells around the trunk, and the tree grows.

What are the xylem and phloem for?
A factory as tall as a tree can't function without elevators to move things up and down. The xylem and the phloem are these elevators:
- The xylem takes water with mineral salts (sap) from the roots to the leaves.
- The phloem sends the sap to all parts of the tree after it's been processed by the leaves.

What are those light and dark rings we see in a cut trunk?
They're the layers that are made as the tree grows. The lighter rings are formed during the spring and summer and are called the early wood; the darker rings are called the late wood because they're formed during the autumn and winter. In parts of the world where seasons aren't so defined, such as tropical climates, the growth rings aren't as easy to see.

What are roots for?

And why do trees push up the sidewalk?

All trees have roots, and all roots have the same functions: to secure trees to the ground, and to absorb water and other substances to feed the trees.

Some trees have roots that grow and grow, up to several yards deep. This is the case with eucalyptus trees, which, because they come from very dry places, find a way to get water wherever they are.

Other trees don't need to search so hard for water, and they have roots closer to the surface of the soil. This is the case with poplars as well as magnolia and ash trees. These are the ones that push up the sidewalk!

✳

Find fantastic trees in botanical gardens!

In many cities, there are botanical gardens and centers you can visit. You can see a wide range of trees from all around the world!

Some examples of special roots

-- -- -- -- -- -- -- -- -- -- --

Most trees have subterranean roots, or roots that grow under the ground. But not all roots grow under the ground.

Aerial roots

Figs are examples of trees that can grow on walls or even on top of other trees. They are able to do this because they have aerial roots, which grow from their trunks until they reach the ground, where they find the water and nutrients they need.

Respiratory roots

Trees that live in places flooded with salt water, such as mangroves (a type of coastal forest in hot places like the tropics), also have to grow special roots. Because these roots grow in underwater soil, they aren't able to find the oxygen the trees need. To solve this problem, the trees developed pencil-like porous roots that grow up from the ground until they're above the water level, where the oxygen is. (Quite a trick!)

*

**Lie on the ground
and look up at all the
leaves of the trees . . .**

. . . you'll see how good and
calm it makes you feel.

Learn to identify a tree

All trees have certain characteristics that define them, such as their height, their color, the shape of their crown, and the kind of leaf or fruit they have. All these aspects are useful for classifying and identifying the tree.

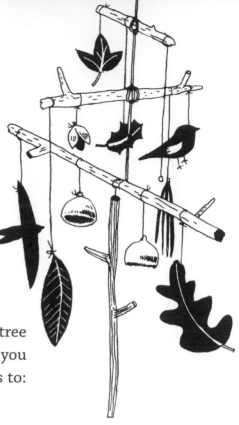

Let's start with the leaves

The first thing you can do to try to identify a tree is look at its leaves. By examining its leaves, you can see which large group of trees it belongs to: the conifers group or the broadleaf group.

For example, pines, firs, cypresses, and yews are conifers. You'll see that their leaves are like needles or overlap like scales. The leaves of these trees are almost always green, and they stay on the trees during the winter. Some of them, such as pines, produce resin, which protects them from insects or fungi.

Oaks and beeches belong to the broadleaf group. Both have wide leaves, and they drop their leaves in the coldest seasons.

When you hold a leaf in your hand, notice if it is wide or thin, hard or soft, and if it's winter, whether it's still green.

What conclusion do you make?

❋
Build a mobile in the shape of a tree

- - - - - - - - - - - - - - - -

Use dry twigs and nylon thread to create the frame. You can then hang a number of items from your "tree": leaves (real ones or ones you've drawn), or anything else you can find in a tree and you want to draw and cut out—butterflies, birds, squirrels, nests, flowers, or fruit.

- - - - - - - - - - - - - - - -

Why are leaves so different from one another?
Even though all leaves serve to capture light from the sun and carry out photosynthesis, the different types of leaves have adapted and have special characteristics according to the places where they first grew.

First of all, pines: because they had to adapt to cold, dry climates, they have leaves that are thin and hard, ones that are hardier and stop water from evaporating so quickly.

And trees from warmer forests, such as Judas trees, poplars, mulberries, or lindens, have wide leaves to enable them to transpire a lot of water.

Leaves: amazing sugar factories!

-- -- -- -- -- -- --

All living things need energy to live.

Animals eat plants or other animals to get energy; trees—and this might surprise you—get their energy from sugar! Sugar is produced in the leaves through photosynthesis. To make it, a tree needs water, mineral salts, carbon dioxide, and sunlight.

The best news for us humans is that when they make their sugar, trees give off oxygen, which we need to live!

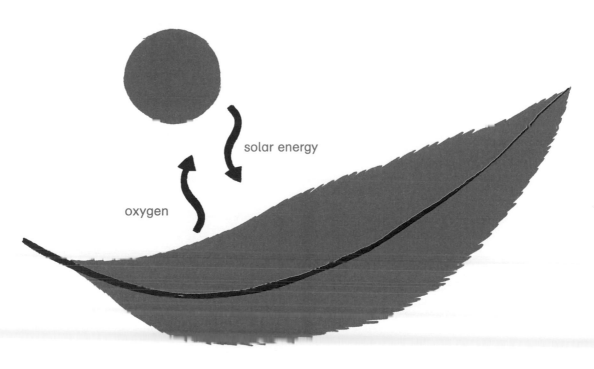

solar energy

oxygen

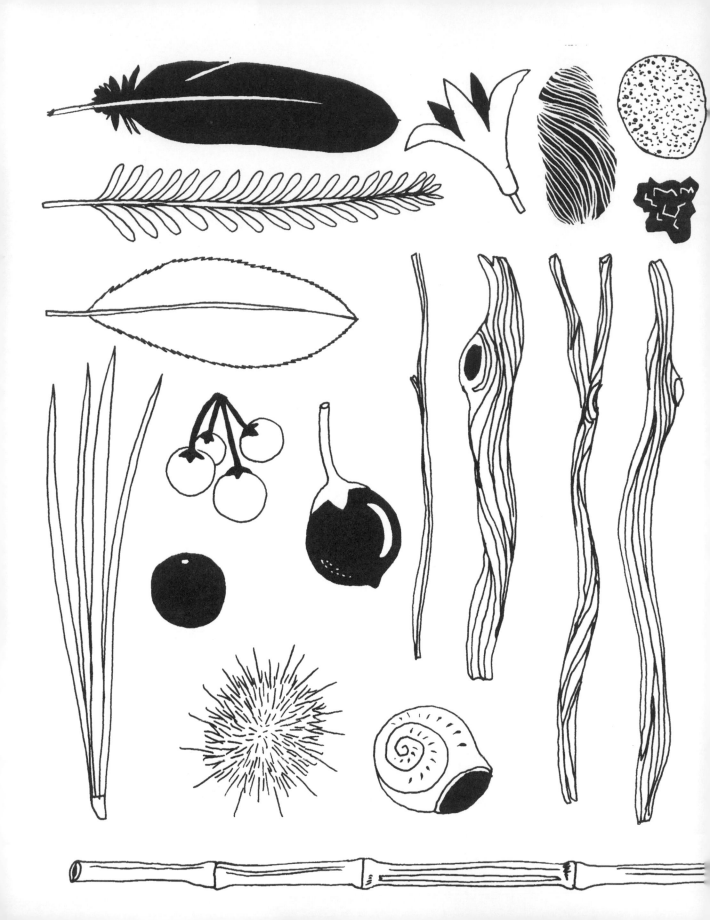

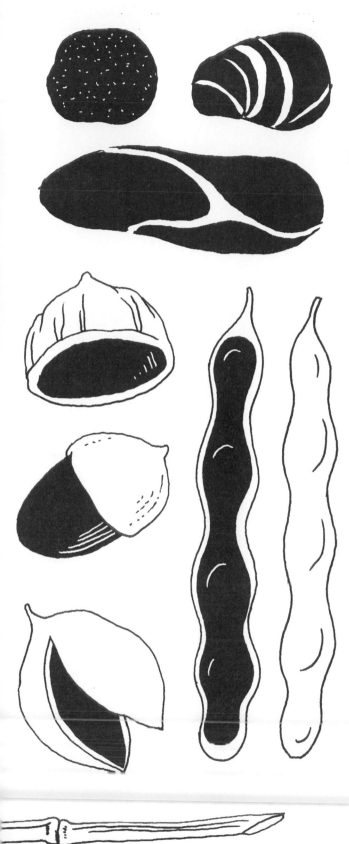

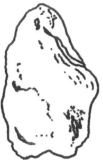

*

**Make sculpture
inspired by Land Art,
or Earth Art**

- - - - - - - - - - - - - - - - - - -

You can use sticks and
other materials from
nature, like leaves,
stones, and soil. If you
need inspiration, look for
images by artists who use
elements of nature in their
work, such as Richard
Long, Robert Smithson,
Alberto Carneiro, Patrick
Dougherty, and Mikael
Hansen.

Why do some trees drop their leaves but others don't?
Tree leaves are sensitive and can freeze and die
when it's cold for a long period of time—and if
the leaves die, the tree dies. But trees have ways
to solve this problem: some species drop their leaves
on purpose when it's very cold and only grow
new leaves when it's warm again. By doing so,
they don't have to constantly replace the
leaves that freeze from the cold and so
save a lot of energy. Other species, like
pines, invest in leaves that are better
able to withstand low temperatures.

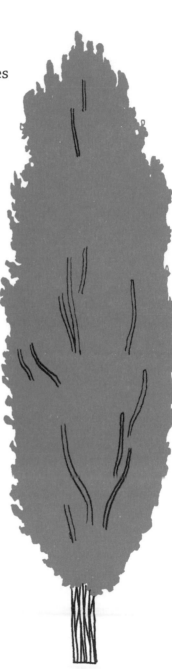

How do trees deal with the changes in the seasons?

- -

Have you noticed that not all trees drop their leaves in the fall?
And that on some trees the leaves turn red and on others they
stay green?

When trees never lose their leaves, we say they're evergreen.
Of course, the leaves of these trees do fall, but only a few at
a time and not during a certain season—new ones are always
growing and we just don't notice. Examples are pines, laurels,
Texas live oaks, and scrub oaks.

When trees lose their leaves in the fall, we say they're deciduous.
Red maple trees and English oaks are deciduous.

When trees keep their dry, reddish leaves in winter, we say their marcescent.
In this case, the leaves only fall when the new leaves begin to
grow the following spring. An example is the northern red oak.

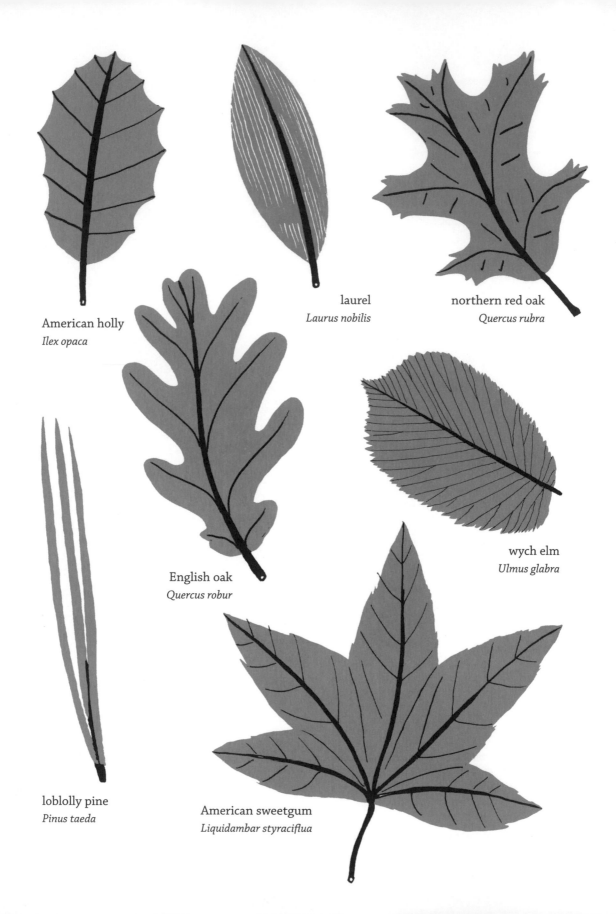

American holly
Ilex opaca

laurel
Laurus nobilis

northern red oak
Quercus rubra

English oak
Quercus robur

wych elm
Ulmus glabra

loblolly pine
Pinus taeda

American sweetgum
Liquidambar styraciflua

ginkgo
Ginkgo biloba

black poplar
Populus nigra

white willow
Salix alba

Pacific yew
Taxus brevifolia

black tupelo
Nyssa sylvatica

honey locust
Gleditsia triacanthos

yellow buckeye
Aesculus flava

Flowers, fruits, and seeds: do all trees have them?

All have seeds, but they're not always packaged in the same way.

Some trees have their seeds inside fleshy, tasty fruit—like pear, orange, or fig trees.

Others have their seeds inside harder fruits—like the walnut, almond, Texas live oak, and scrub oak.

And some trees have seeds that are stored inside fruits that aren't tasty for us humans but that other animals enjoy, such as the fruit of mastic trees, hawthorns, laurels, and many other trees. There are even trees that have seeds that aren't inside fruits, like the cones on pine and fir trees.

❋

An alphabet with twigs (and other items from nature)

- - - - - - - - - - - - - - - -

Look for letters in elements of nature: twigs, stones, patches of lichen and moss, or clouds. Try to find all the letters of the alphabet and make sure to take photos so you have a record of your nature alphabet—there are letters that will inevitably

- - - - - - - - - - - - - - - -

walnut leaves and fruit
Juglans regia

cork oak leaves and acorn
Quercus suber

almond leaves and
fruit
Prunus dulcis

ginkgo leaves and fruit
Ginkgo biloba

laurel leaves and fruit
Laurus nobilis

stone pinecone
Pinus pinea

hawthorn leaves and fruit
Crataegus monogyna

orange leaves, flower,
and fruit
Citrus sinensis

pear leaves and fruit
Pyrus communis

mastic tree
leaves and fruit
Pistacia lentiscus

Why do birds make their nests in trees?

Trees make extraordinary houses for many birds—and for other animals.

Because trees are so tall, many predators can't easily get to the animals' homes. Also, the leaves help to hide nests and protect them from the sun and rain. They also have another function: they're like the birds' "grocery store," where they can easily find lots of fruits and bugs to eat.

Is it a girl or a boy?

Did you know that trees can be male or female? And that sometimes they're both at once? It's true. When a species of tree has some trees that have male reproductive parts and others that have female parts, we say that the species is **dioecious** (like yew, white poplar, and ginkgo trees). When the male and female reproductive structures are on the same tree but different branches, we say that the species is **monoecious** (like cork oak and pine trees).

An important tree

The cork oak (*Quercus suber*) is a very special tree that grows in northwest Africa and southwest Europe—and especially in Spain and Portugal, which are the biggest producers of cork in the world.

What is cork?

Cork is the bark of the cork oak tree that's used to make stoppers for bottles, bags, insulation for houses, and many other things. But of course cork oaks don't make the cork just for us to put in bottles.

What is cork for in nature?

Cork oaks grow in places where the summer is hot and there are frequent fires. The main function of cork is to protect the tree, mainly from these fires. A fire can pass over a cork oak and burn all its leaves, but if it's got cork, the inside of the tree is protected and everything will grow again!

People learned how to take the cork from the trees without killing them, how to extract the cork so, little by little, it will grow back.

Why are there numbers painted on the trunks of cork oaks?

If you've ever seen a cork oak, you've probably seen a number painted on its bark.

This number is there so we know in which year the cork should be removed again. Cork isn't removed every year, only every nine or ten years.

There's a kind of code among cork producers: when they remove the cork, they paint the last numeral of the current year. For example, if the cork was removed in 2014, they paint a 4 on the tree; if it was removed in 2015, a 5, and so on. Because the cork should be removed every nine or ten years, then they know that, if the tree has a 4, the cork should be removed in 2023 or 2024. That way there are no mistakes!

✳

Visit a monumental tree!

Monumental trees are trees that distinguish themselves from others of the same species by their size, shape, age, rarity, or historical interest.

These trees are considered of the public interest and are treated like national monuments. Investigate where you can find some of the most important ones in your area.

Did you know that cork has even been to space?

For many years, cork has been used on NASA's trips to space. This is because it is fire resistant and an excellent insulator. In fact, if you line a whole room with cork, no one outside the room will hear what's going on in there.

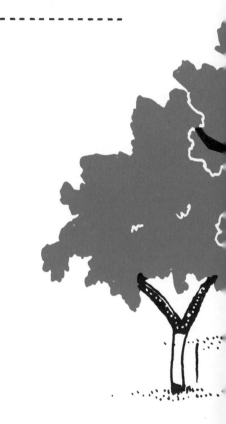

Build a swing and reach the clouds

- -

Here are some tips for your safety and for the health of the tree:

- Choose trees with harder wood (e.g., English oaks, beech trees, or maple).
- Choose branches that are about 20 ft (6 m) off the ground, measure more than 8 in (20 cm) in diameter, and are wide enough that they don't bend when the swing is attached.

- The swing should be about 3–5 ft (1–1.5 m) away from the main trunk.
- The branch has to be healthy. Avoid branches that have any signs of disease, infestation, or cracks, or that have narrow attachments to the main branch. Never use a dead branch—it might break!

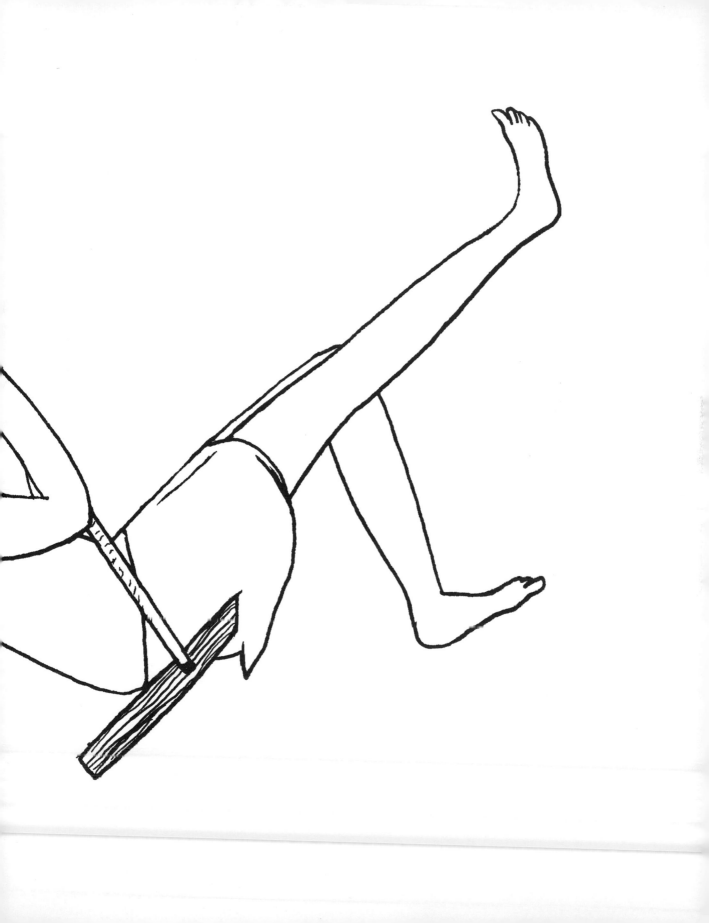

They live in all regions of the planet, the North Pole and the South Pole, mountains and plains, deserts and big cities. They conquered the earth, the sky, and even the waves of the sea . . . They're birds, of course! When we see them gliding high above, we can't help but think . . .

I wish I could fly, too!

What distinguishes birds from other animals?

The thing that makes birds different from other animals is that their bodies are covered with feathers. Nowadays, this is the one characteristic that only birds have. But this wasn't always the case. Millions of years ago, there were other animals with feathers that today we would not necessarily consider birds—certain dinosaurs. Because of this, some scientists believe that birds should belong to the reptiles group.

Who's right?
We don't know, but one thing is certain: birds descended from dinosaurs, specifically from the same group of dinosaurs as the famous *Tyrannosaurus rex*. Scientists have even discovered some similarities between this fearsome predator and . . . the chicken!

The truth is that birds and reptiles today are so different that most scientists put them in different groups.

If it flies is it a bird?
No. There are lots of animals that fly but aren't birds: lots of insects, such as flies and butterflies, and even some mammals, such as bats. But no one flies as many hours straight and as far as some birds, not even most airplanes.

Which bird holds the world record?
One record holder is, without doubt, the bar-tailed godwit, which is able to fly almost 7,500 mi (12,000 km) without stopping (from Alaska to New Zealand). Bar-tailed godwits take about nine days to complete this journey, during which they don't eat or drink.

How can birds fly like that?

Birds manage this feat because their bodies are well adapted for flying.

Bones
Their bones have a lot of hollow space and, therefore, are very light.

Feathers and beaks
Their feathers and beaks are also very light. They are made of keratin—the same material as your hair.

Organs
Their internal organs become smaller so they don't weigh as much when they have to fly many hours on end during migration.

Muscles
Their chest muscles are very strong so they can flap their wings.

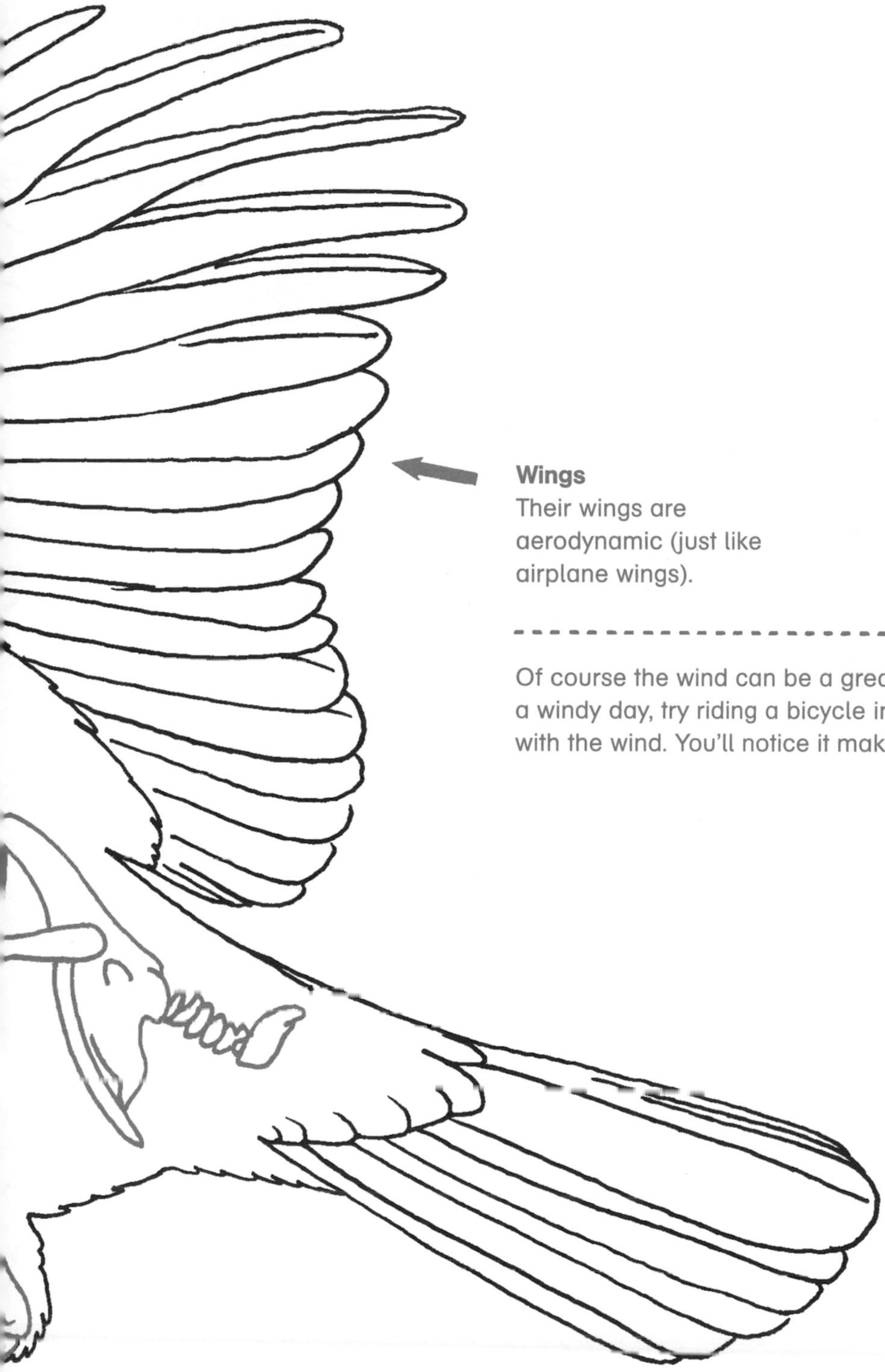

Wings
Their wings are
aerodynamic (just like
airplane wings).

- -

Of course the wind can be a great help for flying. On
a windy day, try riding a bicycle into the wind and then
with the wind. You'll notice it makes a big difference!

What are aerodynamic wings?

Seen from the side (in profile), birds' wings are a half-droplet shape, just like the wings of an airplane. This shape means that when air passes over the wing, the air moves at different speed below the wing and above the wing, which causes lift.

Which is the fastest bird?

The peregrine falcon. When it's hunting in a nosedive, it can fly at over 180 mph (300 kph)! In fact, the peregrine falcon isn't just the fastest bird—it's the fastest animal there is.

- -

And which bird flies the highest?

The species of bird that tends to fly highest is the bar-headed goose. This goose lives in Asia, and during its annual migration, it crosses the Himalayas (the highest mountains in the world).
Scientists put small GPS units on their backs and proved that these geese can fly at an altitude of 23,000 ft (7 km)!

But watch out . . .
The bird that was found flying at the highest altitude was not a goose: it was a Rüppell's vulture, which was flying at 36,000 ft (11 km) and crashed into an airplane flying at the same altitude. The bird died, but the airplane was able to land safely, even though it was damaged.

- -

And which bird flaps its wings the most?

This is, unquestionably, the amethyst woodstar hummingbird. All hummingbirds flap their wings very fast, but this one is able to flap its wings 80 times per second. And all to stay still in front of flowers while it drinks their nectar.

And which bird migrates the farthest?

One of the birds that fly the farthest without stopping is, as you already know, the bar-tailed godwit. But the one that migrates farthest of all is the Arctic tern, which, every fall, flies from the Arctic Sea to the Antarctic. After five years, an Arctic tern will have flown as many miles as the distance between the earth and the moon! This species also holds the record in another category: it is the animal that spends the most time in summer—it's as though it's constantly chasing summer and the mildest temperatures.

If chickens are birds, why don't they fly?

Actually, chickens are able to flutter a bit, and their cousins that live in the wild in Southeast Asia are able to fly for real. But there are some birds that can't even flutter because their ancestors stopped needing to fly and they lost that ability. The most well-known of these are ostriches and penguins.

Where do penguins live?

Penguins live only in the cold waters of the most southerly oceans. But in other regions, there are birds with similar characteristics, even though they're not related to penguins, such as the guillemot and razorbill. These birds haven't lost their ability to fly, but they do dive very deep in the sea like penguins do, and, just like penguins, they look like they're wearing a black tuxedo with a white shirt. Why do you think that is?

When they're in the water with their bellies down, razorbills are difficult for the fish below them to see because their white bellies are easily confused with the surface of the sea, where the light comes from. Meanwhile, they're also difficult to see for the animals that are above them because their black backs are easily confused with the dark depths of the sea. This way they go unnoticed by their prey (when they're hunting) and by their predators (when they try to catch them).

airo

How can there be birds everywhere?

No other animal group is as well distributed around the world as birds. And the key to this success is, once again, their ability to fly.

By flying, birds are able to reach remote areas that few animals can get to. Also, their bodies have adapted to the characteristics of different habitats, and this is why they're different sizes and colors and have different beaks and feet.

Different kinds of feet

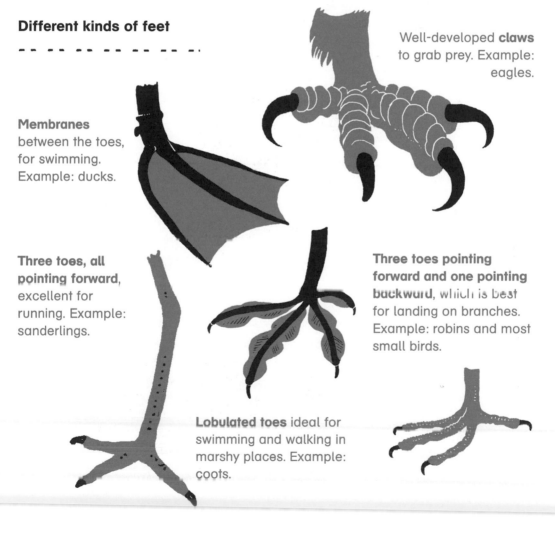

Well-developed claws to grab prey. Example: eagles.

Membranes between the toes, for swimming. Example: ducks.

Three toes, all pointing forward, excellent for running. Example: sanderlings.

Three toes pointing forward and one pointing backward, which is best for landing on branches. Example: robins and most small birds.

Lobulated toes ideal for swimming and walking in marshy places. Example: coots.

Different kinds of beaks

Birds' beaks are adapted to the different kind of things they eat. Some beaks are better for eating seeds, others for catching fish.

Shearwater

Just like the beaks of other marine birds, the shearwater's beak is very well adapted to life at sea. It uses it to catch the fish and squid it eats and, through the small tubes on the upper part, it gets rid of the excess salt from its food.

Hawfinch

The hawfinch has one of the strongest beaks adapted for eating seeds. It is so strong that it can break open a cherry pit!

Woodpecker

The woodpecker has a very strong beak, which it uses to make holes in tree trunks. It then pushes its long, sticky tongue into the holes and is able to pull out insects to eat.

Nightjar

This nocturnal bird eats insects that it catches while flying. To help it do this, it has long, very sensitive bristles around its mouth that help it detect prey in the darkness.

Arctic tern

This bird eats small fish, which it catches by diving from the air. Its narrow beak is adapted for this kind of hunting.

Curlew

Waders, such as this curlew, have long, thin beaks that are very sensitive at the tip, an adaptation for catching small animals that live buried in the mud.

Spoonbill

The spoonbill's beak looks like a spatula to help it eat in the water. This bird's diet is varied and includes mollusks, crustaceans, insects, fish, and even amphibians.

White wagtail

Insectivorous birds, such as the wagtail, generally have very thin beaks, which give them the precision they need to catch their prey.

Duck

Many ducks eat small animals and plants that live in the water. This is why their beaks have very fine whiskers, which filter the food.

Flamingo

The flamingo's beak works like a net: when it dips it into the water, lots of crustaceans and other small animals get trapped in it.

Peregrine falcon

The beaks of birds of prey are very strong and sharp: perfect for tearing the flesh of the prey they feed on.

Where do they choose to make their nests?

Birds are very careful about the places they choose to build their nests. After all, that's where they're going to lay their eggs and where their baby chicks will hatch! Whether it's on the ground, in a tree, in a cave, or in a hole in a garage wall, the most important thing is that the nest is safe from predators.

Types and locations of nests

There are species that make their nests on the ground and surround them with small stones so they're better disguised and protected.

Some make their nests in small caves . . .

. . . others use holes in trees.

Many small birds make nests among the leaves of plants or in the branches of trees. (These nests are normally cup-shaped.)

Some birds take advantage of human structures (for example, utility poles and roofs) to make their nests. This is the case with swallows and storks.

Many species of vulture choose to nest on ledges close to rivers.

How do I put up a birdhouse?

- -

Some important tips:

○ Birds are more likely to move into your birdhouse if you put it in an area with few trees and, most important, few old trees (which are the ones that have the most holes and recesses).

○ The best time to put up your birdhouse is at the end of autumn or the beginning of winter. This is because around the middle of winter, birds start looking for holes to make their nests, and if they find an empty birdhouse, they might choose it!

○ Put your birdhouse in a place protected by branches so that it isn't very exposed, for example, on a branch that's partially covered by vegetation, and protected from the sun. Be careful, too, that the entrance is facing away from prevailing winds. This way, the birds will be better protected from cold, wind, and rain.

○ Put the box at least 10–13 ft (3–4 m) off the ground and facing slightly downward so that rain can't get in so easily and build up inside.

○ Remember that your birdhouse might not be occupied the first spring after you put it up. This can take a while or might never happen: don't forget that it's more likely to be successful when there are fewer old trees nearby.

NOTE: In some cases, it can be useful to put a bit of sand or vegetation inside your birdhouse. If it ends up being occupied, for example, by little owls, which don't make a nest, this will be useful to stop their eggs from rolling around.

blackcap

●

Record the sounds of birds

- - - - - - - - - - - - - - - - -

Choose a place where there are lots of birds and make a recording of the sounds they make. Later on, you can try to identify them from their songs, or you can simply enjoy listening to the recording.

- - - - - - - - - - - - - - - - -

Why do birds sing?

Have you heard a robin sing on a spring morning? Or a blackcap? Birds are famous for their singing. In most species, it's the males that do the most singing. They use their song to attract females, but also to warn other males not to come too close: "Hey, don't come over here—this territory is mine!"

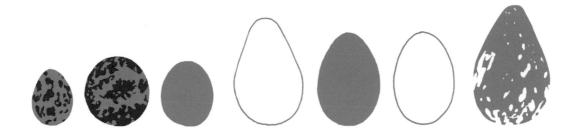

Do all birds lay eggs?

Yes, all birds lay eggs, but eggs from different birds can vary quite a bit. There are big and small eggs, rounder or longer eggs, dark and light, spotted, rough, or smooth. All of them start off having a yolk and a white inside, which, as the days go by, may turn into a chick.

How old are chicks when they leave the nest?

Some chicks hatch in a hurry and full of energy—just a few minutes after they leave the egg, they start running and are already able to eat on their own (partridges, for example). Other chicks stay in the nest for weeks (sometimes months!), being fed by their parents, which rush around trying to find food to bring them, like blackbird chicks, which stay in the nest for between two and three weeks.

Different kinds of eggs

It's often enough to see the color and shape of eggshells to identify which bird they belong to. You have to know which species nest in the area where the eggs were found, and compare them with the pictures in a specialized guide.

What do birds eat?

The answer seems obvious: birdseed, of course! But only some birds (especially the ones in cages) eat this. The ones that live in the wild, the ones we see outside, eat quite a variety of things. Biologists group birds according to what they eat, but this isn't always an easy job. Some birds like to confuse us and eat different kinds of food according to what they like or what is available. Here are some examples of how they are generally divided:

Granivorous and frugivorous birds (the "vegetarians") eat mainly seeds and fruit. Example: sparrows.

sparrow

flycatcher

Piscivorous birds eat mainly fish. Examples: kingfishers and ospreys.

Insectivorous birds eat insects, spiders, or worms. Examples: flycatchers and bee-eaters.

bee-eater

osprey

kingfisher

peregrine falcon

The peregrine falcon: a success story

Peregrine falcons exist almost all over the world, and can be seen both in the country and in urban areas—they sometimes even makes nests in buildings in big cities. But it wasn't always this way. In the middle of the last century, the peregrine falcon was a species in danger of extinction.

The main causes of their decline were direct hunting or poisoning by use of pesticides in agriculture, such as DDT. But scientists discovered what was happening in time, and thanks to conservation efforts we can still admire this species, which is among the most amazing predators of the animal kingdom.

As you already know, the peregrine falcon is the fastest animal that exists. There's only one reason it flies so fast: it feeds almost exclusively on other birds, which it catches mid-flight. This is why it has to be faster than its prey.

Peregrine falcons are also well known for the incredible migrations they make: some fly up to 9,300 mi (15,000 km) every year, between the places where they reproduce and spend the winter. When they're traveling, they can cover up to 118 mi (190 km) in a single day.

Other facts about peregrine falcons:
- They're very faithful birds: when they choose a mate or territory, it's for life.
- They can be found in a variety of habitats—deserts, tundras, tropical zones, and cities.
- Females lay between three and four eggs, which are incubated by both males and females.

How do I identify species of birds?

You will need:
A pair of binoculars
A field guide to identifying birds
A notebook
Colored pencils

- Start in the nearest yard or garden. On a sunny morning, nice and early, go out and observe the birds that fly by and also those that land on the ground, a post, a shrub, or a branch.

- If you have binoculars, you'll be able to see some details. Notice the size of the bird, its coloring, the size and shape of its beak and feet, and its behavior: is it singing? Is it looking for something? Is it standing still or hopping around?

- Notice, too, if it's alone or in a group with other birds.

- Try to hear the song: How would you characterize it? High pitched? Deep? Continuous? Does it have breaks? What does the song sound like?

- Then look in your field guide for the birds you saw. Some species are very similar, and at first, it might seem difficult to distinguish them. But with experience, you'll see that it gets easier and easier.

Why are there only swallows in spring?

Just as we sometimes take summer vacations far away from home, there are many species of birds that decide to make a long journey to a faraway place once a year. But birds make this journey in order to survive: some because they can't bear the cold; others because there's no more food in the places they live (perhaps due to snow); other birds journey for both of these reasons. This journey is called migration.

Where do birds migrate to?
Some migrate nearby, but others can migrate to the other side of the planet.

Are there migrant birds outside?
Yes, there are. Depending on where do you live, and on the season, so you can find different species. For example, ducks and waders usually breed in Northern latitudes, such as the arctic and sub-arctic regions, and move to warmer places to spend the winter months. During this period you can find them in wetlands and coastal areas of most temperate regions. Many small birds prefer to spend the winter in the Southern hemisphere, and return to breed during spring. Some famous examples are the swifts, the swallows, and the cuckoos.

swallows and swifts
Can you tell which is which?

great spotted cuckoo

Endangered species

Humans and birds have a long history, but birds don't always come out on top. Many species of birds are becoming extinct due to the destruction of their habitats, hunting, or illegal capture.

Vultures and bustards are two particularly endangered groups of birds.

●

Do you want to help save the birds from extinction?

- - - - - - - - - - - - - - -

Around the world, there are more than 1,300 species of birds in danger of extinction. But fortunately, there are also lots of people concerned with guaranteeing their survival.

You can help, too, directly, by participating in conservation work, or indirectly, by talking to your friends and classmates about efforts to help these species.

If interested, contact a nature conservation organization. (See the list at the end of this book.)

- - - - - - - - - - - - - - -

bustard

vulture

Are you interested in seeing a migration?

Even though birds don't stay very long during a migration (since they're only passing through), it's relatively easy to spot them.

Keep these tips in mind:

- August and November are the best months to see migratory birds, but April and May can also be good.

- During migration periods, there are migratory birds everywhere, but you'll see the biggest groups of birds at estuaries and lakes.

SOME SPECIES
YOU CAN
SEE IN THE
OUTSIDE WORLD

small white
Pieris rapae

monarch
Danaus plexippus

small copper
Lycaena phlaeas

common blue
Polyommatus icarus

swallowtail
Papilio machaon

silver-spotted
skipper
Epargyreus clarus

clouded yellow
Colias croceus

grayling
Hipparchia semele

great spangled fritillary
Speyeria cybele

painted lady
Vanessa (Cynthia) cardui

pipevine swallowtail
Battus philenor

eastern tiger
swallowtail
Papilio glaucus

red admiral
Vanessa atalanta

meadow brown
Maniola jurtina

orange-tip
Anthocharis cardamines

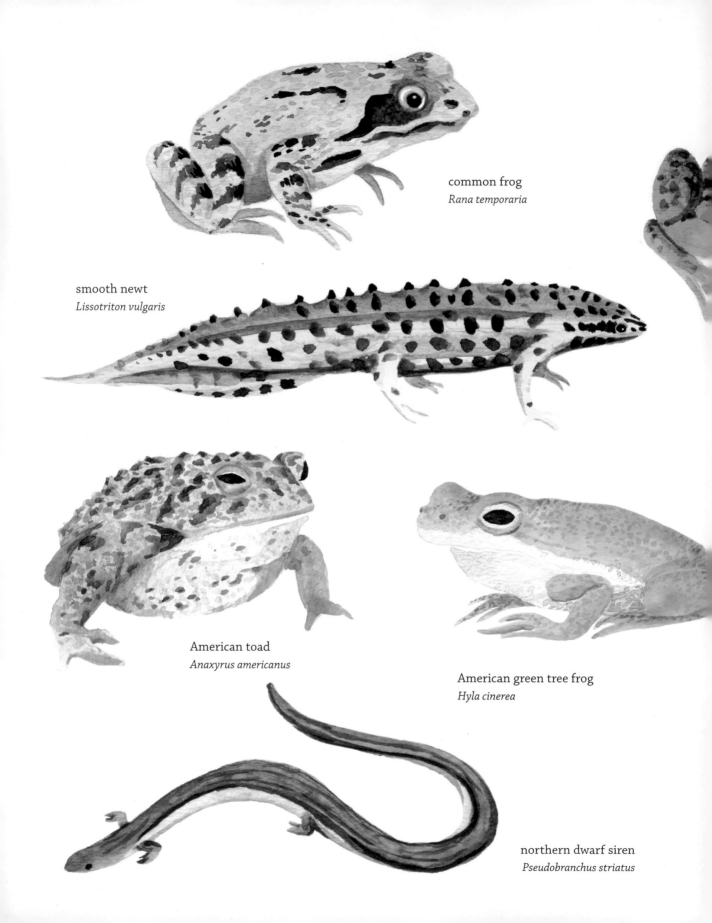

common frog
Rana temporaria

smooth newt
Lissotriton vulgaris

American toad
Anaxyrus americanus

American green tree frog
Hyla cinerea

northern dwarf siren
Pseudobranchus striatus

plains spadefoot
Spea bombifrons

American bullfrog
Lithobates catesbeianus

fire salamander
Salamandra salamandra

natterjack toad
Bufo calamita

common toad
Bufo bufo

pecan
Carya illinoensis

coast redwood
Sequoia sempervirens

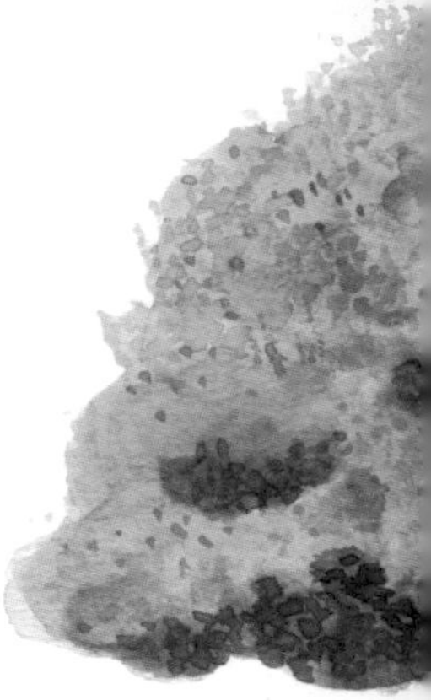

Silver birch
Betula pendula

crack willow
Salix fragilis

bur oak
Quercus macrocarpa

sugar maple
Acer Saccharum

sweet chestnut
Castanea sativa

eastern white pine
Pinus strobus

red cedar
Juniperus virginiana

alder
Alnus glutinosa

tamarack
Larix laricina

downy birch
Betula pubescens

common house martin
Delichon urbica

collared dove
Streptopelia decaocto

house sparrow
Passer domesticus

barn swallow
Hirundo rustica

common kestrel
Falco tinnunculus

common swift
Apus apus

mallard
Anas platyrhynchos

common starling
Sturnus vulgaris

golden eagle
Aquila chrysaetos

Canada goose
Branta canadensis

robin
Erithacus rubecula

barn owl
Tyto alba

mourning dove
Zenaida macroura

blue jay
Cyanocitta cristata

long-eared owl
Asio otus

dark-eyed junco
Junco hyemalis

blackbird
Turdus merula

red-winged blackbird
Agelaius phoeniceus

black-capped chickadee
Parus atricapillus

grass snake
Natrix natrix

sand lizard
Lacerta agilis

eastern kingsnake
Lampropeltis getula

adder
Vipera berus

American alligator
Alligator mississippiensis

western banded gecko
Coleonyx variegatus

common lizard
Zootoca vivipara

slowworm
Anguis fragilis

Gila monster
Heloderma suspectum

pond slider
Trachemys scripta

horned lizard
Phrynosoma spp

Carolina anole
Anolis carolinensis

short-headed garter snake
Thamnophis brachystoma

sunflower
Helianthus annuus

primrose
Primula vulgaris

columbine
Aquilegia canadensis

foxglove
Digitalis purpurea

lords-and-ladies
Arum maculatum

cranesbills
Geranium sp.

oxeye daisy
Leucanthemum vulgare

tickseed
Coreopsis spp

field bindweed
Convolvulus arvensis

spear thistle
Cirsium vulgare

poppy
Papaver rhoeas

lupine
Lupinus perennis

bluebell
Hyacinthoides non-scripta

mouse-eared bat
Myotis spp.

red fox
Vulpes vulpes

gray squirrel
Sciurus carolinensis

raccoon
Procyon lotor

red deer/elk
Cervus elaphus/canadiensis

badger
Meles meles

gray wolf
Canis lupus

hedgehog
Erinaceus europaeus

European otter
Lutra lutra

rabbit
Oryctolagus cuniculus

red squirrel
Sciurus vulgaris

mole
Talpa europaea

beaver
Castor spp.

pipistrelle
Pipistrellus/Parastrellus

brown bear
Ursus arctos

wild boar
Sus scrofa

barnacle
Chthamalus spp.

brown algae
Fucus spp.

common octopus
Octopus vulgaris

snakelocks anemone
Anemonia spp.

sea snails
Gibbula spp.

common prawn
Palaemon serratus

blue mussel
Mytilus edulis

sea slug
Felimare fontandraui

brittle stars
Ophiothrix spp.

sea urchin
Strongylocentrotus spp.

limpet
Patella/Lottia

common eelgrass
Zostera marina

shore crab
Carcinus maenas

hermit crab
Pagurus spp.

beadlet anemone
Actinia equina

combtooth blenny
Blenniidae

starfish
Asterias spp.

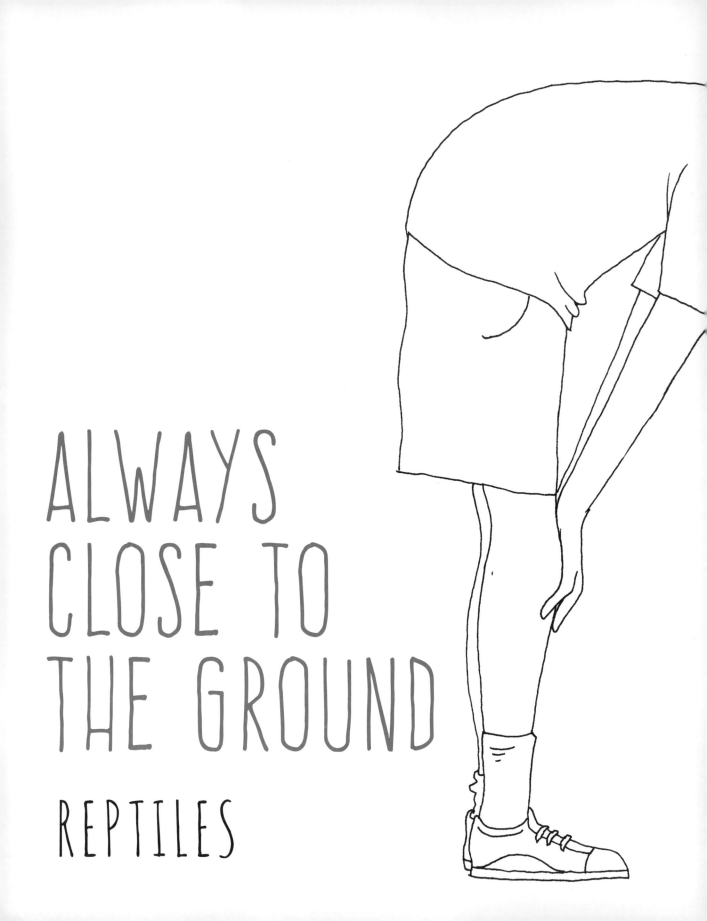

ALWAYS
CLOSE TO
THE GROUND

REPTILES

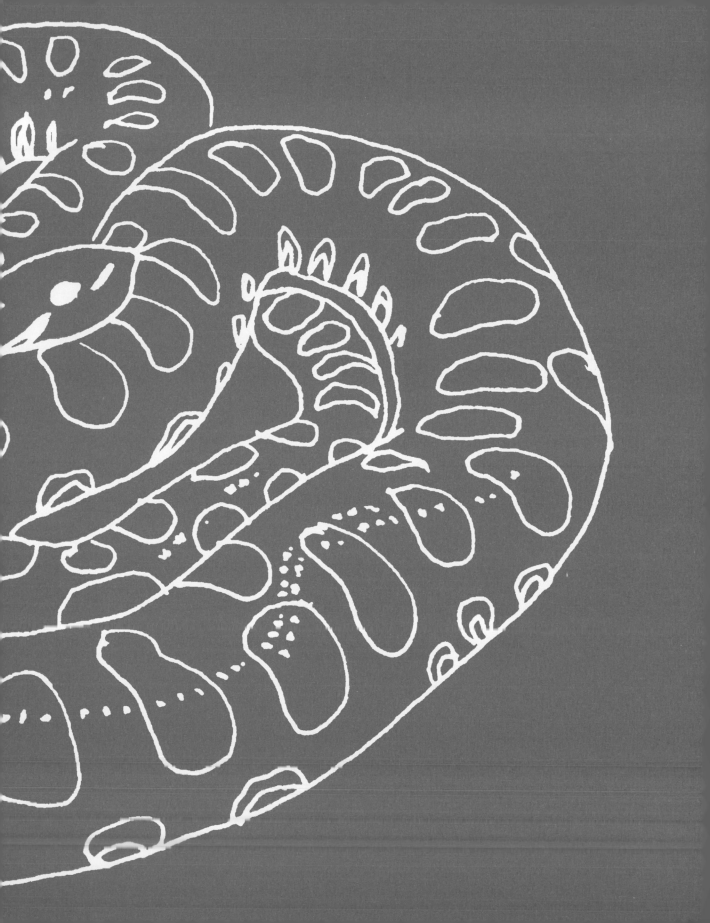

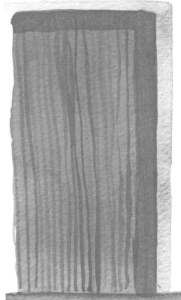

The word reptile comes from the Latin *reptile*, which means "one that creeps." Lots of people are frightened (maybe even terrified!) of this group of animals. But with the exception of some with poisonous venom, there's no real reason for us to be afraid of them.

Find them outside . . . always close to the ground (or perched on a wall).

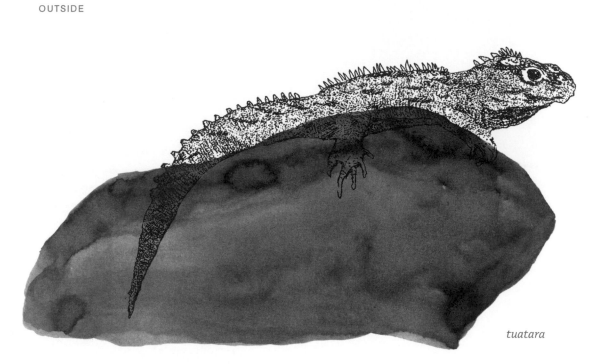

tuatara

What are reptiles?

We say these animals are cold-blooded, but if we touch them in the spring or summer, they can feel very warm. This is because reptiles are animals whose body temperature varies according to the temperature of their environment: their bodies don't produce their own heat (like our bodies do)—it comes from external conditions.

Before it eats breakfast, a reptile needs to warm up, or else it won't have enough energy to catch food. That's why we so often see lizards sitting in the sun! Biologists call these animals ectotherms.

Unlike amphibians, reptiles spend most of their time on land and not in the water. That's why their bodies need scales—so they don't dehydrate and lose too much water.

To sum up: a reptile is a cold-blooded animal with a body covered in scales, and it almost always creeps along the ground.

Show me your scales!

What are scales made from?

Reptiles' scales are made from keratin, which is also the material that our hair and nails, as well as birds' feathers and beaks, are made of.

Are reptile scales the same as fish scales?

No, they're slightly different: reptile scales are made from the most superficial, or outer-most, part of the skin (the epidermis), and fish scales are made from the deepest part of the skin (the dermis).

Are all scales the same?

Some reptiles, for example snakes, lizards, and geckos, have small scales, but turtles and tortoises have large scales called <u>scutes</u> (1).

Chameleons have scales that look like small bumps, called <u>granular</u> scales (2).

Adders and water snakes (*Natrix* spp.) have <u>keeled</u> scales (3), which are divided down the middle by a line that sticks up slightly. (This is one of the reasons why these two species are so often mistaken for each other.)

The large psammodromus, a kind of sand lizard, has <u>imbricate</u> scales (4), which overlap one another slightly like tiles on a roof.

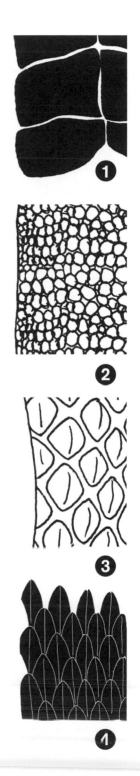

What are they?

There are lots of different reptiles around the world. They are put into groups based on what they have in common. The tuatara, crocodile, and turtle and tortoise groups are the oldest. All the other reptiles are more recent, but they resemble one another and belong to a large group called Squamata.

Turtles and tortoises

This is the oldest group of reptiles in the world—it has existed since the time of the dinosaurs! It includes sea, land, and freshwater turtles. Examples: European pond turtles and red-eared sliders.

Worm lizards

Reptiles in this group look like big worms, but they have a spinal column and scales.

Tuataras

This group only has one genus of reptile: the tuatara, which only exists in New Zealand. It's another very old group. (Also, they have a special characteristic you'll learn about soon.)

Snakes and vipers

This group includes all snakes, poisonous or not. Examples: adders and kingsnakes.

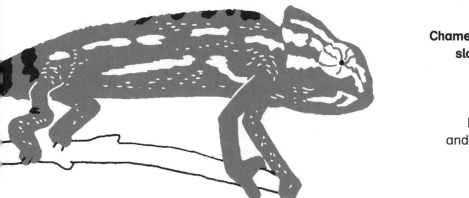

Chameleons, geckos, lizards, slowworms, and western three-toed skinks

This group includes the most species. Examples: sand lizards and common chameleons.

Crocodiles

This group is made up of only crocodiles, which, just like turtles, have lived on our planet for millions of years.

Hylonomus lyelli

How long have they been around?

Reptiles have been around on Earth for more than 300 million years!

A reptile called *Hylonomus lyelli* is the oldest that has been found so far. (Scientists are always discovering new things, and tomorrow there could be a "new" oldest.)

From these first reptiles came all others, a process that took millions of years. Charles Darwin called this evolution. Many reptiles that evolved from this first group are already extinct, as is the case with dinosaurs, but there are others, such as tortoises, that are as old as the dinosaurs and still around!

●

Look at (real) dinosaur footsteps!

- -

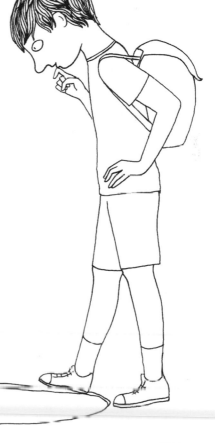

Dinosaur tracks can be found in many places!

The longest continuous set of dinosaur footprints in the world can be found in Colorado along the Purgatoire River. The footprints were made in the late Jurassic period by dinosaurs that include Iguanodon, Apatosaurus, Coelurus, and Triceratops.

Some of the best-known dinosaur footprints on Earth are in Glen Rose, Texas, by the banks of the Paluxy River. These tracks were made by large sauropods, two-legged carnivores, and some smaller two-legged herbivores. There are even some small footprints that look as though they could have been made by humans – but in fact they belong to small, bipedal dinosaurs.

In the UK, you can see fossilized footprints at low tide on Brook Beach, on the Isle of Wight.

- -

Egyptian mongoose

What do they eat? And what eats them?

Most reptiles are carnivores, but some tortoises and large lizards, such as iguanas, are vegetarians or omnivores. Some snakes almost always eat eggs; others prefer to eat other reptiles.

But reptiles are also food for a lot of animals. This is the case with the short-toed snake eagle. Mongooses love eating snakes, too, and some snakes love eating chameleons. Even we humans eat reptiles: in some countries, people eat crocodile steak, turtle soup, stuffed snake, and lots of other delicacies.

Defense strategies (and some theater . . .)

Because they have a lot of predators, reptiles invented a sort of theatricality to defend themselves—biologists call this defense strategies. Depending on the danger, reptiles act out one of their favorite scenes:

- They inflate their bodies to seem larger than they actually are.
- They open their mouths wide and make threatening noises.

- They disguise themselves as whatever is around them, as chameleons do. This is called mimicry.
- They imitate more dangerous species. For example, the viperine snake holds its head so it looks like a viper and even attacks like a viper.
- They pretend to be dead. When they feel threatened, viperine snakes lie still and leave off a horrible smell.
- Lots of lizards and geckos drop their tail, which can keep moving on its own and look like an animal wriggling. When the predator goes to grab the tail, the lizard can take the opportunity to escape.
- If none of the other tricks work, they bite . . .

How many eyes do reptiles have?

Reptiles have two eyes plus an extra one: the pineal eye. This eye is found on the top of the head, right in the middle, but it isn't used for seeing anything: it just gives the animal an idea about the light that's around it. The reptiles with the most developed pineal eyes are the tuatara, which, as you know, are a very old species that live in New Zealand.

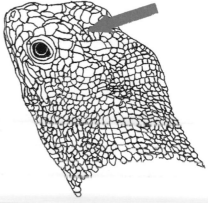

**Speaking of
crocodiles . . .**

-- -- -- -- -- --

The world's largest reptile
is the saltwater crocodile
(*Crocodylus porosus*), which
can grow up to 23 ft (7 m)
long and weigh over 3,300 lb
(1,500 kg).

And before the egg?

-- -- -- -- -- --

You need a male and a
female to make an egg.
Each one has its own kind of
seed to make other reptiles.
For the male, this is called
a spermatozoid, and for the
female, it is called an ovule.
When the two come together,
they form an egg. You might
be thinking, *But that's how it
always is!*

But is it? Actually no. There
are always exceptions. And
lizards are proof of this. In
certain places, there are
only female lizards, and
they're able to make eggs
using only their own ovules!
The problem is that all the
lizards come out identical to
their mother and no males
are ever born. This is called
parthenogenesis.

How are baby reptiles born?

Almost all reptiles are <u>oviparous</u>, meaning their babies are born from eggs. The eggs are normally buried in the ground, and when the babies are born, they're ready to start their lives on their own.

Very rarely, like with some crocodiles, females make nests, lay the eggs, and stay to look after them until the babies are born (and even afterward, when the babies are still very small).

There are some reptiles, like vipers, that don't lay eggs: the babies grow inside the egg, inside the mother's belly, and the egg only comes out when the baby is born. (These animals are <u>ovoviviparous</u>.)

There are also species such as many skinks, which are <u>viviparous,</u> and produce living young.

Nasty as a snake!

People often portray reptiles as unpleasant: they say snakes are evil and poisonous, and that geckos are poisonous and their skin is sticky. There are even stories that people swear are true, but are nothing more than folktales. (You can read one of these stories on the left.)

Do reptiles deserve this reputation?

Of course not! Most reptiles aren't sticky or poisonous—there are exceptions, but these are rare. Their scaly skin is dry and not moist. In fact, snakeskin is very silky and even pleasant to the touch. (But never touch a snake in the wild if you see one!)

All living things have a function in their environment, and reptiles are no exception. Have you ever thought what would happen if reptiles disappeared? There could be a big increase in lots of other species, and this would cause an imbalance in nature. For example, geckos eat a lot of mosquitoes, and snakes eat a lot of rats: if there were no geckos or snakes, the number of mosquitoes and rats would go up tremendously!

For people who like scary stories . . .

- - - - - - - -

Some Europeans say they know somebody who died from drinking from a cup a gecko had fallen in. That's nonsense! Geckos aren't poisonous, and if they do fall off the roof (and land in a cup), it's just because they've been up there hunting insects . . .

Do you know what a herpetologist is?

It's a scientist who studies reptiles and amphibians. The word herpetologist comes from the Greek *herpeton*, which means "reptile." At first, herpetology was a science that studied only reptiles, but later it changed to include amphibians as well (the first group of vertebrates to live out of water).

Pretend you're a herpetologist

Go on an outing to the countryside to try to find some species. Bring a camera so you can take your time to identify what you find. (You can look at the pictures later.) Make a list of all the reptiles you see (on that day and on others).

Tips:
When to look?
The best time to look, without a doubt, is springtime, when it's sunny. In winter, it's very cold and these animals hibernate; in summer, they hide away during the hottest hours.

Where to look?
The best way to see them is when they come out to sunbathe. Look on walls, stones, tree trunks, or other objects in the sun.

Which are the easiest to see?
Lizards are the reptiles that are some of the most common and easiest to see.

Tricks:
- Try attracting a lizard with a little stick with honey or some fruit on it. Wait patiently and the lizard should come closer.

- Some reptiles, such as geckos, go out at night and sleep in the day, so to see them, you can look in the evening. In summer, geckos appear on the walls of houses, mainly underneath lights, waiting for insects.
- You can also look for geckos in the daytime, when they're resting in dark and peaceful places (e.g., mailboxes).

Shall we pop over to an island?

When an animal arrives on an island for the first time, everything is different: there might not be the same species as on the mainland, there might not even be predators that want to eat it—and this can obviously be an advantage. If nothing wants to hunt it, the animal leads a more relaxed, longer life and this change can mean that its behavior alters.

With time, if the animals on the mainland and those that moved to the island are separated for many years, different species may develop. Evolution at work once again!

For example, in Madagascar, which is an island on the east side of the African continent, there are over 300 species of reptiles and over 90% are endemic. Because Madagascar is a large island that has been isolated for millions of years, the reptiles that live there have been isolated from their relatives on the continent for all this time, which has given rise to different species.

The difference between native and endemic species

-- -- -- -- -- --

Native species are species that naturally exist in a region or ecosystem. In other words, they exist without anyone having taken them there, but are not exclusive to that region (they can be native to other places).

Endemic species are native species that only exist in a given region of the planet, they don't naturally exist anywhere else in the world.

How did animals get to islands, which are surrounded by water?

Some animals arrived during the Ice Age, when much more water was frozen, and the sea level was lower. And so some of the places that are islands today were originally linked to the mainland and were easier to reach!

Other animals—mainly those on islands a long way from the coast—were carried there on a boat (this often happened with mice and rats) or were taken there on purpose by humans. For example, humans have taken rabbits to islands. The rabbits reproduced very quickly and became an invasive species that had a big impact on the ecosystem.

There are even cases of animals that arrive on islands by flying, swimming, or using floating vegetation as a raft. In other words, all on their own, without human intervention.

Go to an island and see special lizards and geckos (and other animals, of course!)

- - - - - - - - - - - - - - - -

A planet with so much water, like ours, also has a lot of islands and islets. What about visiting one? Choose one close to your home (if you live near the sea) or take advantage of a vacation and persuade your parents to take you to one. It's best to choose one that's wilder so you can see more species (lots of islands are nature reserves). Don't forget to take comfortable shoes, a hat, a camera, and binoculars (to see the birds). Follow the tips in "Pretend you're a herpetologist". If there are no reptiles there, you can always pretend you're an ornithologist!

- - - - - - - - - - - - - - - -

wall lizard

Some brave it and take a dip in the ocean

Marine iguanas live on all the islands of the Galapagos archipelago. When Charles Darwin arrived at this archipelago and saw the marine iguanas for the first time he thought they were so ugly that he called them "disgusting clumsy lizards"! In fact, these reptiles do look a bit strange and they behave a bit strangely for a lizard, too: they're the only ones that eat in the ocean, eating seaweed.

Because they're ectothermic, their bodies cool down when they go to eat so they have to get back onto land to warm up in the sun. They're normally dark colored and this helps them absorb heat. (When you wear a black T-shirt and go out in the sun, doesn't it make you hotter?)

Other reptiles that like salt water

There are other reptiles that live in the ocean and never get out. This is the case with sea snakes, like the yellow-bellied sea snake.

Others, like sea turtles, live in the sea and only set foot on land to lay their eggs. This the case with the leatherback sea turtle. The females choose a beach in the area where they were born and lay their eggs—normally more than a hundred of them! Meanwhile, once the males have hatched and entered the water, they never get back on land again.

These leatherbacks are the biggest turtles that exist on Earth—they can grown up to 7 ft (2 m) long, and can weigh more than 1,500 lb (700 kg)! They mainly feed off jellyfish, and while they breathe air and come to the surface to take in oxygen, they can hold their breath and remain underwather for up to 85 minutes.

leatherback sea turtle

Chameleons

Chameleons are reptiles with very peculiar characteristics, which make them look strange and funny at the same time. Although they can vary in size, from 1 in (3 cm), up to 25 in (63 cm), they have a lot in common.

Most chameleons—especially the bigger species—have a long prehensile tail, which grabs things as if it was another hand; protruding eyes that can move in different directions at the same time; and a long tongue with a sticky tip. If a chameleon sees an insect, it stares at it, slowly gets ready, and fires its tongue. As soon as the tongue touches the insect, it sticks to it and moves back into the chameleon's mouth (but all this happens so fast that it's hard to see with the naked eye).

What is it that everyone knows about chameleons?
That they change color, of course! But why?

There are various reasons why chameleons change colour:
- To disguise themselves: chameleons's patterns make it more difficult for predators to find them in vegetation, so they're better protected.
- To thermoregulate (change their body temperature): when their bodies are cold, chameleons can turn darker, and because dark colors absorb more light, this makes them heat up more quickly when they're in the sun. The craziest thing is when chameleons are able to turn one side of their bodies dark and the other light!
- To "dress" according to their mood: the colors and patterns also depend on a chameleon's mood and are used to communicate. For example, when a female is pregnant she has a different pattern to warn males that she doesn't want to be with them anymore.

Courting chameleons

It's true chamleons like courting, but they also like to change partners—in other words, both males and females can mate with more than one partner. Some males even walk miles in search of a new female! The female chooses whether or not to accept him, if she thinks that he's more colorful or has showier horns than her other partner.

Eggs grow inside female chameleons's bellies for three to six weeks: at the end of this time they're ready to be born! Some chameleons are born directly from their mothers's bellies (viviparous), but most species are oviparous. In this case, the mothers look for a good place to bury their eggs. They dig a deep hole—and because the mothers have little feet, this job can take more than a day! After the hole is finished, they lay the eggs and cover everything carefully. This is such a big effort that it's common for them to die shortly afterward. The eggs stay buried for several months until the baby chameleons start to climb out. They all come out at the same time, and dig up to the surface and quickly try to find a tree to climb. Then their big adventure begins!

Does everything in nature serve a purpose?

Flowers could simply be pretty things for us to look at . . . but in reality, flowers aren't just attractive parts of plants: they play a very important role in the life of the plant.

What could that role be?

Get ready for a world of colors, smells, and buzzing sounds . . .

Where are they?

Everyone knows about colorful flowers like roses, carnations, tulips, lilies, and marigolds. But not all flowers are as big and brightly colored.
Some are so small and inconspicuous that we can only see them with the help of a magnifying glass. There are others that grow without anyone having planted them—we find them in meadows, vegetable gardens, or even in cracks in the sidewalk . . .

In <u>gardens and yards</u>, there are some flowers that aren't native to the area— they have been planted in places around the world simply because they're beautiful, for instance, roses, pansies, hibiscus, and dahlias.

In <u>vegetable gardens</u>, you can find squash, watermelon, melon, and cucumber flowers. And also onion, carrot, or passion fruit flowers (which are hermaphrodites and have the reproductive organs of both sexes).

Flowers can appear in some <u>unexpected places</u>. If you're in a town or city, you might see small

dahlia

plants growing in cracks in the sidewalk—we usually call these plants weeds. These plants also have flowers.

On the walls or roofs of buildings, there can even be flowers, such as white stonecrop, navelwort, and Kenilworth ivy.

On pavements and paths, you might see clover, prickly sow thistle, field mustard, or blue pimpernel.

Where there is a bit more soil, you might see Bermuda buttercup, milk thistle, dandelions, Cornish mallow, musk storksbill, daisies, or poppies.

In the countryside, you can see bushes that have flowers, like species of rockrose, heather, rosemary, or French lavender.

Environmentally-friendly sidewalks?

You might think the spaces and cracks in sidewalk are small. But if we added up all the soil in these spaces, we'd have a really big area! Many plants and critters live here. Also, this soil is important because it lets water through—otherwise the water wouldn't filter back into the ground.

Pansy
Viola x wittrockiana

Hibiscus
Hibiscus rosa-sinensis

Pumpkin flower
Cucurbita pepo

Onion flower
Allium cepa

French lavender
Lavandula stoechas

Passion fruit flower
Passiflora edulis

Watermelon flower
Citrullus lanatus

Kenilworth ivy
Cymbalaria muralis

Carrot flower
Daucus carota

Muskmelon flower
Cucumis melo

Cucumber flower
Cucumis sativus

White clover
Trifolium repens

Heather
Calluna vulgaris

Prickly sow thistle
Sonchus asper

Rosemary
Rosmarinus officinalis

Hawkbit
Leontodon taraxacoides

What are flowers for?

Flowers exist so plants can reproduce—in other words, they exist so new plants can grow.

How did flowers appear in the world?

Flowers are made from modified leaves. Millions of years ago, when there weren't yet flowers, some plants started to very slowly change their leaves, until they transformed into the flowers we know today.

Why do flowers smell so good?

People normally really like the smell of flowers. But it's not *us* the flowers want to attract with their lovely smell: flowers are designed to attract animals, normally insects, that can take their pollen to another flower of the same species and pollinate it.

What is pollination?

Pollination is the transfer of pollen from the stamen to the gynoecium. This meeting generates the seeds—the baby plants.

When pollination takes place inside of a flower or between two flowers of the same plant, it is called self-pollination. When it happens between flowers of different plants, it is called cross-pollination, which is more common. In cross-pollination, the plants need help (usually from insects or the wind) to reproduce, and to get this help, they use certain tricks . . .

✳

Identify the parts of a flower

- - - - - - - - - - - - - - - - - -

Identifying the parts of a flower isn't easy because some flowers are close together on the same base, and so the different parts are very small and/or difficult to identify.

Tips:

- Collect flowers from various plants, preferably big ones, because they're easier to identify.

- Carefully separate the various parts of flowers and try to identify them according to the diagram on the next page.

- You'll see that flowers can be very different depending on species, but it's most common to have several stamens and colored petals and for the gynoecium to have one pistil.

- - - - - - - - - - - - - - - - - -

Corolla
The corolla is the name for all the petals together.

Gynoecium
The gynoecium is the female part of the flower. It's formed by carpels, which produce the ovules.

Androecium
The androecium is the male part of the flower. It's formed by the stamens, which produce the pollen.

Petals
The petals are the colored parts that attract insects.

Calyx
The calyx is the name for the sepals, the small green parts that protect the flower when it's still a bud.

What's the main trick for attracting insects?
It's a sweet trick . . . Some insects, such as bees, feed off nectar, the sugary liquid that flowers produce in addition to pollen. While the bees are collecting the nectar, the pollen sticks to their legs, and when the bees fly away and land on other flowers, they leave the pollen behind—and pollen is needed for fertilization.

Some flowers smell quite pleasant, but some produce horrible smells, like the smell of rotting meat. Instead of pretty butterflies, these flowers are attempting to attract flies, insects that love stinky things!

✳ **Make a crown of flowers**

- -

You can make a crown of flowers by twisting together daisies. Gather several with long stems of about the same length. Take two flowers, cross the stems, and twist them together. Add more flowers, in a circlular shape, until you make a crown the size of your head.

Not everything is as it seems

(other tricks plants use to attract insects)

- -

Flowers that imitate insects

There are flowers that don't just have colorful petals to attract pollinators. Some, like orchids, have transformed their petals and sepals so they look like insects. There are some orchids that look like a particular species of insect, and only that species can pollinate them.

Flowers with runways

To guarantee that animals find the pollen and nectar, some flowers have a kind of line drawn on them to show the way. These lines aren't always visible to us, but for the insects, which have a different kind of vision than we do, these lines really stand out.

orchid

tulip

Petals that aren't petals

Some flowers have "almost" petals—these flowers have found a way to imitate a pretty corolla by making their sepals very large and colorful so they look like petals. This is the case with tulips and lilies. There are plants that go even further, having leaves as colorful as a large flower. The bougainvillea is an example of this. Try looking inside this "false flower," and there you'll find the real (and very tiny) white flowers, tucked inside the colorful leaves.

And after the flower?

Flowers turn into fruits, which are able to protect the seeds and also attract animals by how they look, smell, and taste. Why is this so important?

Because it's quite likely that a seed hidden inside of a tasty fruit will be eaten by an animal. And later, when it's time for that animal to poop, it's also likely that the animal will be far away from the plant where it picked the fruit . . . And so the plant meets its goal: to spread its seeds without its offspring growing too close to it and competing for the same resources (soil, light, water, and nutrients).

✳

Make envelopes for seeds

- - - - - - - - - - - - - - - -

Gather seeds from various plants. Leave them out to dry and then keep them in pretty origami envelopes that you can label and decorate with drawings. Collect them or give them as presents.

Take a close look at a daisy

Look at a daisy, with a magnifying glass if you can.

How many flowers do you see? Just one? Really?
If you look closely, the middle part is made of lots of tiny flowers—so many you can't even count them! The outside has larger petals and gives us the impression that we're looking at a single flower with a large yellow "eye."

<u>Really, what we looking at isn't a flower. It's an inflorescence—a lot of flowers grouped together.</u>

There are other "flowers" that have this feature: marigolds, dahlias, chrysanthemums, and gerberas. These all have a kind of inflorescence (called a capitulum) and belong to a large family called composite flowers.

These flowers don't have to do as much work because only the ones on the outside have to spend energy making big petals to attract pollinators. But in the end, they all benefit.

● **Make a poppy dancer**

- -

You can make a delicate dancer by bending the petals of a poppy down toward its stem and tying them with a bit of grass or a thin stem to make the "waist."

Then push a stick up through the part that will be the dancer's body. You can move the stick to make your poppy dance.

Note: The hardest part is to turn the petals downward without tearing them off—the petals are very fragile.

✳ ✳

Make a bouquet of wildflowers

Have fun combining colors, shapes, and sizes to make a pretty bouquet. You can tie it with any natural material that will work as a ribbon. **Then give someone your bouquet!**

- - - - - - - - - - - - -

Stop and smell the roses (and all the other flowers!)

When you walk through the countryside or a garden, close your eyes and try to notice the different smells in the air. Can you identify any of them?

When we think of mammals, we might first think of an enormous lion or tiger! But big, hairy animals aren't the only ones in this group. Mammals can be enormous or very tiny, really hairy, almost bald, or even spiky. They can have legs, fins, or wings. They can swim in water, walk on land, or fly through the air . . . (And don't forget: humans are also mammals!)

So how are we all alike?

Where do we come from?

Mammals can be so different from one another that it's hard to believe they belong to the same group. But millions of years ago, there was an ancestor common to all of us . . .

What was this ancestor?

That ancestor belonged to a group called *Cynodontia*, which includes animals similar to reptiles and from which various species emerged. Some of these species are already extinct, but others evolved into other mammals that are alive today. In 2013, scientists made a model of this animal, common to all placental mammals. Although they can't be sure, they think this animal looked a bit like a shrew and ate insects. The oldest mammal fossils that have been found are of this species, but the case isn't closed just yet.

What happened next?

In a world full of very diverse environments—oceans, tropical forests, deserts, and frozen tundras—mammals have adapted so they can live in almost all of these places. Over millions of years, they acquired wings for flying, changed arms into fins for swimming, or grew lots of hair for protecting themselves from the cold—and these are only a few examples. Think of how different mammals are from one another!

Some mammals went *splash*!

Perhaps because there were already a lot of animals on land and there wasn't much to eat, some species started to use the oceans to find food. As time went by, they spent more and more time there and constantly adapted to life in the water. Over the course of millions of years, their arms turned into fins, their legs became a tail similar to a fish's, and their bodies took on a shape that made it easier to move through the water. This is how there came to be whales, dolphins, and seals, which are all aquatic mammals very well adapted to life in the water.

Do whales have noses?

Like all mammals, marine mammals breathe using lungs. (They have to come to the surface of the water to breathe.) Whales don't breathe through noses, but they do have a sort of nostril: a blowhole, which is on the top of their head. Whales breathe through there, and it's where that famous spurt of water comes out . . .

Do you know which animal has the biggest brain in the world?

The sperm whale! Its brain can weigh up to 20 lb (9 kg).

It's also the largest known mammal with teeth, the largest carnivore, the noisiest animal (it spurts water out of its blowhole up to over 30 ft [10 m] high!), and the best diver (it dives to over 6,500 ft [2,000 m])!

The sperm whale is the king of records!

Some mammals still prefer land

(but they decided to dig!)

Many mammals live on land, and there are some that even live underneath it! Moles, for example, dig long tunnels that lead to their burrows, where they sleep and have their babies. To dig the tunnels, they push the soil out and up to the surface, forming mounds, like the ones you can see in the country or in gardens.

Do you know how moles keep their food fresh?
Moles love eating worms. So that they always have worms available, moles bury worms in their burrows and bite the worms so they're paralyzed. This way the worms are alive but can't escape!

The Pyrenean desman: an endangered species
There is a kind of mole that lives in water instead of under the ground: the Pyrenean desman, which is very rare (only existing in certain parts of Portugal and Spain) and in danger of extinction. This mole lives in rivers where the water is clean and has small waves. It's very sensitive: if the river where it lives gets polluted or altered somehow (for example, by a dam), the Pyrenean desman will have to leave and find a new home.

Is it a ball of fur or a mole?

Pyrenean desmans are not easy to find because they leave their burrows only at night (the best time to hunt in the water).

The Pyrenean desman measures about 8 in (20 cm) in length and looks like a ball of fur.

Its fur is waterproof and keeps it warm. When the mole swims underwater, its fur gets a kind of metallic shine.

It has a trumpet-shaped snout, which never stops moving!

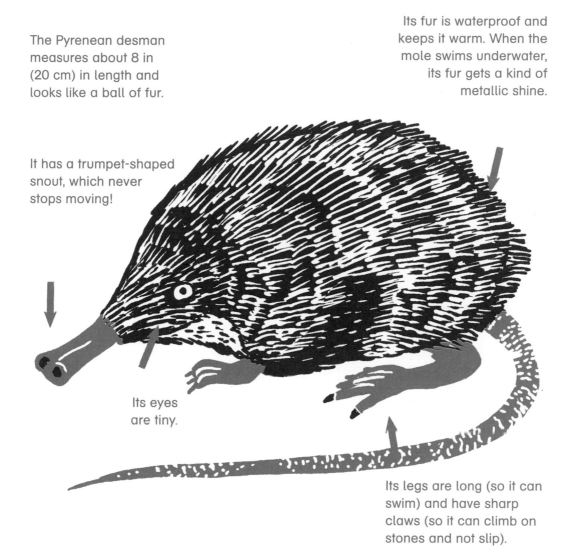

Its eyes are tiny.

Its legs are long (so it can swim) and have sharp claws (so it can climb on stones and not slip).

During the day, it can eat half its body weight in insects and other critters. That's a lot of food!

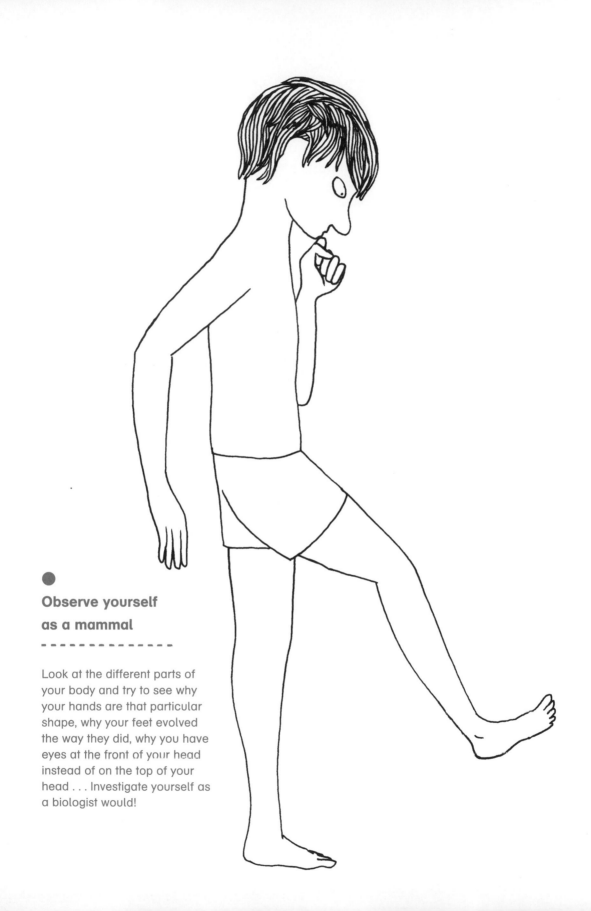

Observe yourself
as a mammal

- - - - - - - - - - - - - -

Look at the different parts of
your body and try to see why
your hands are that particular
shape, why your feet evolved
the way they did, why you have
eyes at the front of your head
instead of on the top of your
head . . . Investigate yourself as
a biologist would!

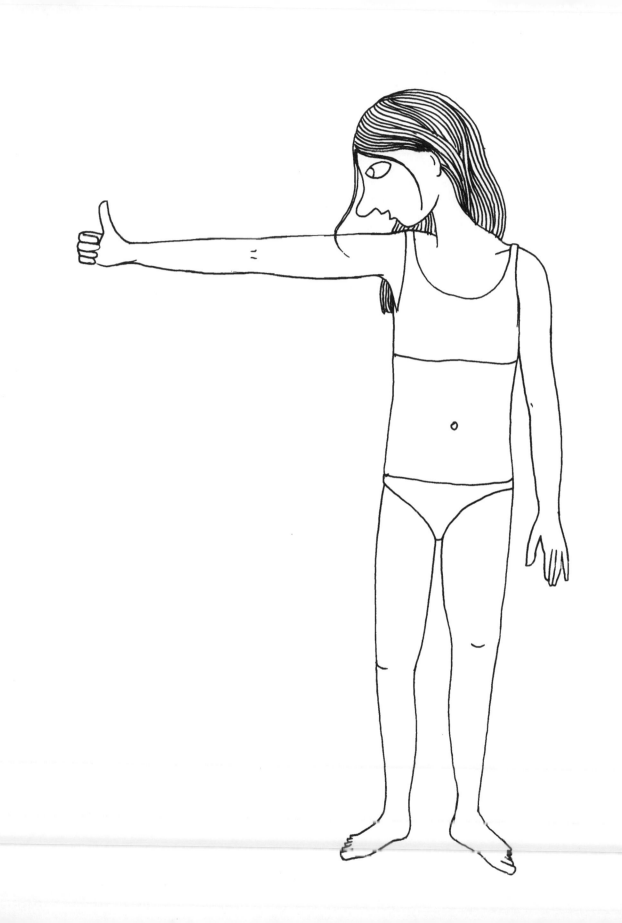

Mammals that fly above us

There are terrestrial mammals that hardly ever walk on land and instead
spend a lot of time flying: bats!

Are there bats where I live?
It's quite possible! At night, especially on warm nights, you can see
bats flying around streetlights in many towns and cities. Maybe you've
already seen one but didn't realize it was a bat—they can be very small
and very fast!

Have you noticed how bats' wings are similar to our arms?
Just like us, they have upper arms, forearms, and hands.

How do they manage to fly without bumping into things?

Even though bats have eyes and can see well, they also use their ears to find their way and avoid obstacles when they're flying. Bats make various sounds that we can't hear. These sounds move through the air as a wave, and when these waves meet an object, they bounce back. When these sound waves return to the bat, their ears transmit this information to their brain, which can then sense everything in front of it. This is called echolocation. <u>Note:</u> There are bats (flying foxes) that only use their eyesight.

Why do bats sleep hanging from their feet?

Bats' ancestors were animals similar to shrews that walked on four legs. As these animals evolved, their front legs turned into wings and the knees on their back legs changed so they bent backward. Because of this, their legs are rather weak, so bats aren't able to stand on them (unlike birds, for example, which have stronger legs). Also, if they're hanging, bats are able to fly off more quickly.

So why don't bats fall when they're sleeping?

When we hang from the branch of a tree, we have to hold on tight with our hands. When we relax our muscles, our hands open and we fall to the ground. With bats, it's the other way around: when their muscles are relaxed, their feet close; and when they want to open their feet, bats have to make an effort to do so. That explains why their feet will never open when they're relaxed and sleeping!

How are mammals born?

Mammals are not all born in the same way. Biologists—who like classifying and giving things names—decided to group mammals according to the way they're born.

Placental mammals

These mammals grow inside their mothers' bellies, where they're fed through an umbilical cord until they're developed enough to live outside of their mother. Most of the mammals we know of belong to this group. Examples: dogs, rats, bats, dolphins, tigers, hippopotamuses, wolves—and humans, of course!

Monotreme mammals

These mammals lay eggs that their babies hatch from, and just like all other mammals, the babies drink their mother's milk! This is the group with fewest species, and they exist only in Australasia. Examples: echidnas and platypuses.

Marsupial mammals

The females have a kind of pouch outside their bellies, called a marsupium. The babies are born very small, and with their eyes still closed, they climb into the marsupium. The mother's teats, full of milk, are in there, and the babies feed and grow. These animals mainly exist in Australasia and South America. Examples: koalas and kangaroos.

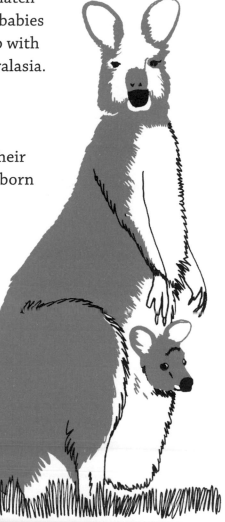

- -

What am I?
I have the beak and feet of a duck,
  but I'm not a duck.
I have the body of an otter,
  but I'm not an otter.
I have poison, but I'm not a snake.

The **platypus**! This animal is so strange that the first time a stuffed specimen was brought from Australia to Europe, biologists thought that it was a hoax and that someone had stuck together parts of different animals! As well as having feet and a beak like a duck and a body like an otter, a platypus lays eggs. The male has a poisonous spur on each hind leg.

Have fun mixing animals

- - - - - - - - - - - - - -

Take inspiration from the platypus and invent funny animals, mixing parts of different animals. Then you can make up names for your creations.

Do all mammals have fur?

Yes, but we can't always see it. Some only have fur when they're inside their mothers' bellies and when they're born the hair falls out, as is the case with dolphins. Other animals, like some whales, have completely bare skin and only a few hairs on their heads. Or it could be that the fur had transformed into spines that protect the animal from predators— like hedgehogs, porcupines, and echidnas (1)—or hard plates, like pangolins (2).

There are also mammals with so much fur that even the palms of their hands and feet are covered. This is the case with polar bears   , which have to stay warm in very cold climates.

There are some mammals that don't like to always wear the same "clothes," such as the Arctic hare (4), which has a brown summer coat and a winter coat that's white as snow! This way, it's always well disguised, whatever the season.

Can mammals be carnivores *and* herbivores?

Of course. Being defined as a mammal is related to what the animal eats right after it's born—its mother's milk. Later, when the animals grow, the different species have very different diets: some eat insects (and are called insectivores), some eat plants (and are called herbivores), and others eat a bit of everything (and are called omnivores, like us).

"Would you like a bite?" ask the carnivores
When we think of carnivores, we may think of big animals like lions, tigers, or killer whales. But there are also much smaller mammals that are brave predators, for example, weasels, which are able to catch rabbits, animals much bigger than they are.

Very cunning omnivores
Some primates, such as chimpanzees, eat animals and vegetables, and because they're so intelligent, they're able to use simple tools to help them feed themselves. For example, if they want to eat fruit that has a hard shell, they use a stone to break it; if they want to eat ants, they use a stick that they push into the anthill to make the ants scurry out. After that, all they have to do is enjoy the snacks!

- -

Did you know that the Etruscan shrew (*Suncus etruscus*) is one of the smallest mammals in the world? It's just 2 in (5 cm) long, and is a greedy predator!

Are there wolves out there?

Well, it depends where you live . . . But don't worry, even if there are wolves in your region, they aren't going to appear in front of you in a city! Wolves always hide away in the most isolated places and don't like getting close to us.

Across the world there are two species of wolf: the gray wolf and the red wolf. The gray wolf once lived almost everywhere on the planet, and was the most widely distributed mammal (except humans, of course!). It's now extinct in lots of European countries, Mexico, and most of the USA, due to being hunted by humans. It was worse with the red wolf, and this species became extinct in the wild in 1980. Luckily, there were still red wolves in captivity and it was possible to reintroduce this species in North Carolina (USA), one of the places where it originally existed.

Do wolves talk, too?
Apart from the big bad wolf in the story of Little Red Riding Hood, no wolf can speak . . . but, even so, wolves communicate very well with one another, not only by howling (when they howl they can be heard, even at a distance, by other wolves) but also through scent and vision. Marks of excrement and urine and also "scratches" (holes made using their claws) are made for other wolves to see and smell.

Do you know what a pack is?

- - - - - - - - -

It's a family of wolves, normally made up of a father, mother, and youngest offspring (and sometimes the older ones, too).

Once a year, in April or May, each she-wolf has about 5 cubs per litter. When these offspring are 1 or 2 years old, they leave their parents and form another family.

What color is the gray wolf?

- - - - - - - - - -

This isn't a trick question! The gray wolf can be white with gray, brown, black, cream, or tawny colors and sometimes almost entirely white or black. But, as you can tell from the name, gray is the most common color.

And what about biologists, do they howl, too?

Yes! Biologists who study wolves howl to see if a wolf responds. Because wolves don't like unknown wolves being in their territory, they'll answer any howl just to say: "I'm in charge here, go and howl somewhere else!" So biologists can tell that there are wolves in that area. A good trick, isn't it?

Do you want to know a story about bears?

Everyone knows that bears like honey. In the past, lots of people had beehives to provide them with honey. So, as soon as bears smelled the honey, all they thought about was "attacking" these hives!

This is why, when there were lots of bears in Europe, people built huge walls over 10 ft (3 m) high around beehives. That way the bears couldn't go on their greedy attacks.

Today, there aren't bears in many of these countries, but there are still a lot of traces of their paths in some place names, for example: Bear Hole, Bear Creek, Bear Wood, Bear Valley. Even though they're extinct in many countries in Europe, North Africa, and Asia, brown bears are still common in many Eurasian countries and in North America. There are also seven other species of bear, with the giant panda being the most endangered of all.

Write a book of animal stories

After having read this chapter (and all the other ones about animals) you might have come up with a lot of ideas for stories inspired by the lives of animals. Write and illustrate your ideas.

Draw different mammals

Of course it's not easy to find mammals in nature that will stay still long enough for you to draw them. So, find images and try to draw different animals in this group, looking carefully at their different shapes, legs, mouths and coverings. Drawing is also a way to better understand the things around us.

TO THE CENTER OF THE EARTH

ROCKS

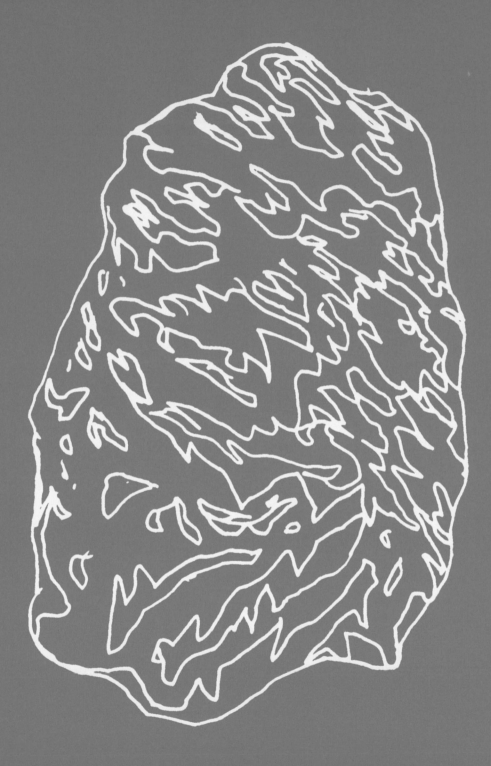

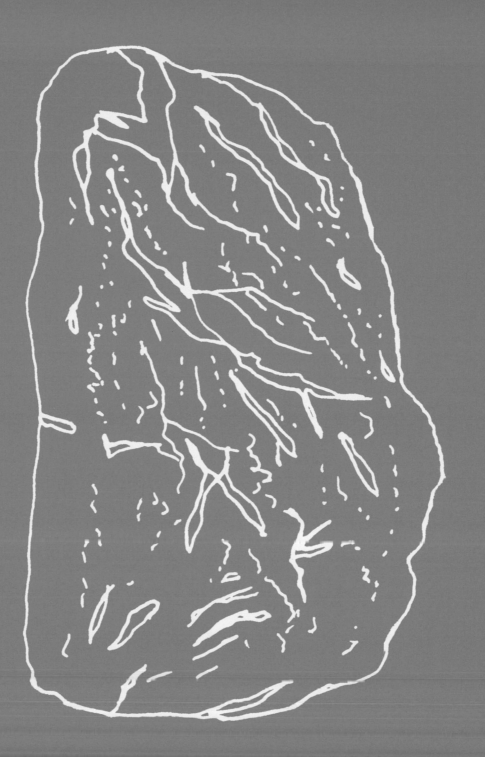

When you're out for a walk, think about this: under your feet, down at the center of the earth, are giant chunks of rock that are millions of years old!

Silent, strong, and mysterious, nature is always there.

Planet Earth or planet Rock?

People say that planet Earth could be called planet Water because it has a lot of water on its surface, but it wouldn't be wrong to call it planet Rock because it's mostly made of rock. Rocks are formed of minerals that combine in different ways, which creates rocks with different properties.

On Earth's surface, the rocks are in a solid state. But down in the planet's core, there's molten rock bubbling away . . .

Blop, blop, blop!

What are rocks?

The rocks you see all around—on the beach, in rivers, on mountains—are mixtures of minerals joined together to make a solid.

Cement and bricks aren't rocks: they're—very impressive!—man-made creations.

Examples of rocks include granite, limestone, basalt, marble, schist, and sandstone.

- -

If Earth was an egg, its crust (on the surface) would be the shell. This shell is covered with water, ice, soil, sand, vegetation, animal and plant remains, etc. Dig down a bit, and soon enough we hit the rock that covers the whole planet.

Mineral + mineral = rock?

Almost all rocks are formed of two or more minerals. For example, granite is a combination of the minerals quartz and feldspar. (It also contains mica but in a smaller amount.) But it's not enough to put two or three minerals together to make a rock . . .

<u>A rock recipe:</u> You have the ingredients (in this case, the minerals), and you'll use these to make a cake (the rock). To make a particular kind of cake, you have to have the ingredients in the right amounts. Then you have to mix and beat the ingredients and heat or cool them, transforming them or cooking them at a precise temperature. The same thing happens with rocks.

And finally, what are minerals?

There are over 4,000 minerals on Earth, all made from chemical elements (oxygen, carbon, etc.) combined in different ways. Quartz, for example, the most abundant mineral on the planet, is formed of two chemical elements: silica and oxygen.

So what are stones?

What we call stones or pebbles are smaller pieces of rock that have broken off from the "bedrock." A lot of the time, as with larger rocks, these smaller stones change shape and texture through weathering and erosion (by water, wind, or temperature, for example) and can become round and smooth, like some you'll find by the ocean or a river.

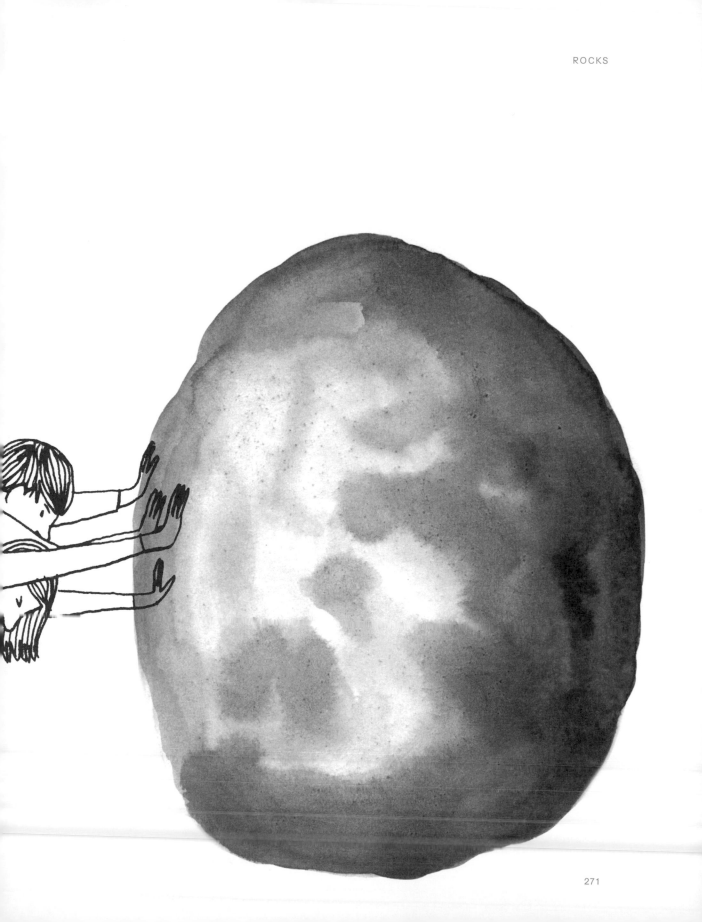

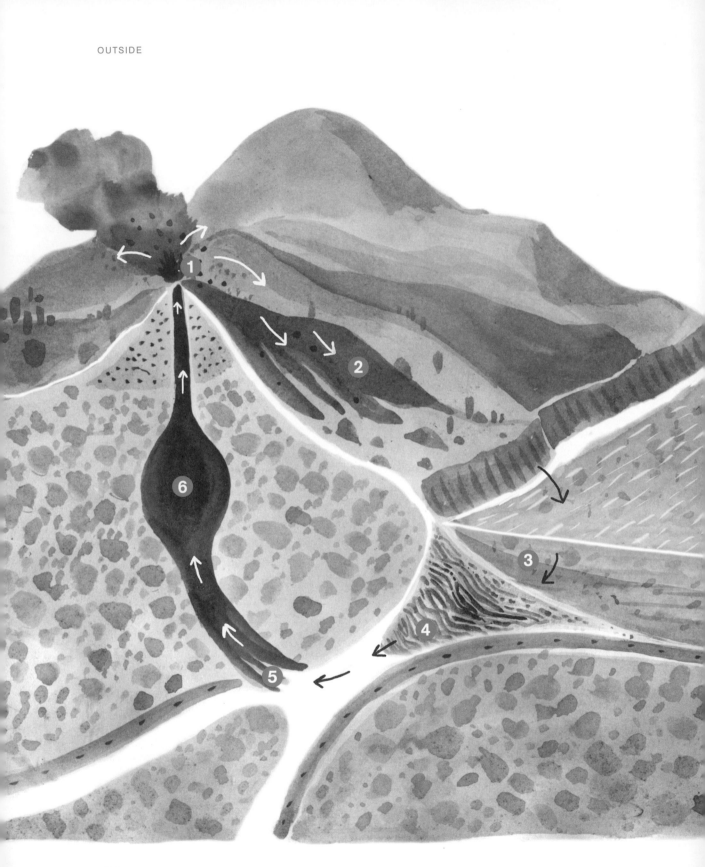

Nature: a great big rock-recycling machine

The materials that make up rocks are never "lost"—they're always changing and being transformed (just like water in the water cycle).

With rocks, this cycle can take thousands or even millions of years.

The movements of the earth (caused by different pressures and temperatures) push solid or liquid magma to the surface and create <u>igneous rocks</u> (1).

(2) <u>On the surface</u>, some of these rocks are split into pieces by weathering and erosion, from variations in temperature and water, wind, etc.

Some of these sediments are transported, deposited, compacted, and consolidated (whew!) creating <u>sedimentary rocks</u> (3).

The movements of the earth keep on going, pressing and heating these rocks, forming <u>metamorphic rocks</u> (4).

Some rocks return to the <u>earth's interior</u> (5). When they melt again, they form <u>magma</u> (6) once more . . .

And a new cycle begins.

What kind of rock are paving stones?

Some countries, like Brazil and Portugal, are famous for their patterned sidewalks with designs and pictures in black and white. This traditional style of paving is called a Portuguese pavement, and it is usually made with blocks of limestone (for the white stones) and basalt (for the black stones). Depending on the region and the availability of geological resources, paving stones can vary. In some areas, paving stones are blocks of granite.

Rock hard! (Are there minerals in my body, too?)

Of course. You know by now that in nature things are always moving and influencing one another. The same thing happens with the minerals that make up rocks: minerals get into underground water (aquifers), surface water (like rivers, streams, and lakes), and seawater, as well as soil, where trees, vegetables, and fruits grow. When we eat and drink, our bodies, which are also part of nature and part of this chain, receive the minerals we need to live. We couldn't live without rocks and minerals!

What is the hardest rock out there?

There is a scale that measures the hardness of minerals. It's called the Mohs scale of mineral hardness, and it measures how easily a mineral is scratched by another. From the softest to the hardest:

- talc (easily scratched by a fingernail)
- gypsum (can be scratched by a fingernail)
- calcite (can be scratched by a copper coin)
- fluorite (can be scratched by an iron nail)
- apatite (can be scratched by glass)
- feldspar (can be scratched by a penknife)
- quartz (can be scratched by a steel blade)
- topaz (can be scratched by a file)
- corundum
- diamond

The hardness of a rock depends on the level of hardness of the minerals it's made from. With this scale, now you know that the champion of hardness is the diamond!

Is there rock that can float?

- - - - - - - - - - - - - - - -

Yes, but only one. Pumice stone is a volcanic rock formed when molten lava (which is rich in gases) is projected into the atmosphere and cools, forming a rock that looks more like a sponge because it has lots of holes. It's the only stone that floats because it's a lot less dense than water. Get a pumice stone (you can easily buy these) and do experiments in water.

- - - - - - - - - - - - - - - -

What is this stone I found?

- - - - - - - - - - - - - - - -

That depends on the area where you found it! And it also depends on the characteristics of that stone. To discover which family of rocks it belongs to, you have to look at your stone closely and find the answers to some questions:

- What color is it?
- Is it made from grains of different colors?
- Can you see any large crystals?
- Is it smooth or rough?
- Is it shiny?
- Is it very hard or does it crumble?
- Does it easily split into layers?
- Is it permeable or impermeable?
- Does it float?

By looking at the next pages, you might be able to come to some conclusions about your stone.

- - - - - - - - - - - - - - - -

Properties of some rocks

Limestone
- Light colors
- Hard
- Dense texture
- Variable permeability
- Doesn't crumble, but splits easily
- Reacts with acid

Granite
- Speckled, various colors
- Hard
- Grainy texture
- Low permeability
- Doesn't crumble or split easily

Clay
- Brown, yellow, green colors
- Can be molded when wet
- Cracks when dry
- Fine-grained texture
- Impermeable
- Crumbles easily

Schist
- Dark colors (gray, brown)
- Not very hard
- Layered texture
- Variable permeability
- Splinters easily

Basalt
- Dark colors (black)
- Very hard
- Very fine grains
- Low permeability
- Doesn't break easily

Marble
- Variable colors (white, gray, pink, etc.)
- Very hard
- Smooth texture
- Impermeable
- Doesn't crumble or split easily
- Reacts with acid

Note: Do not experiment with rocks and chemicals unless a responsible adult is supervising!

sandstone

schist

slate

limestone

coal

granite

gabbro

conglomerate

basalt

Do rocks move?

We're used to thinking of rocks as immobile, stable things. Is this right?

In actual fact rocks do move all on their own—especially the ones that form our planet's crust. They move so slowly and gradually that we hardly ever notice, except when these movements are bigger and cause earthquakes or tremors. But even most earthquakes are so weak that people don't feel them, they're only picked up by seismographs (machines used by scientists to detect movements in the ground).

Do continents move too?

If the rocks that form our planet's crust are moving, that means the continents move too. Approximately 175 million years ago, there was just a single supercontinent, called Pangea, surrounded by a single ocean, Panthalassa. This supercontinent started to separate into smaller continents, which kept moving very slowly, until they arrived in the

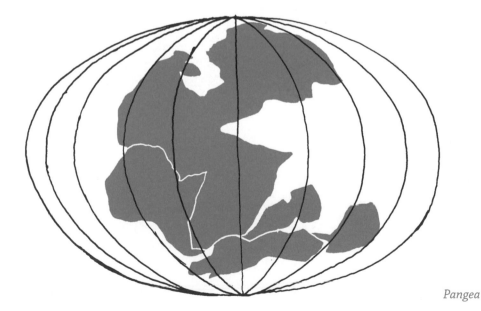

Pangea

positions we know today. And the continents are still moving now. For example, America and Eurasia are moving away from one another: they move about $^3/_4$ in (2 cm) per year in opposite directions—which means that the Atlantic Ocean is getting wider, and the Pacific Ocean is getting narrower.

How do we know that the continents moved (and are still moving)?

Today there are GPS machines (which work in the same way as the GPS in a car) that measure the speed that continents are moving. But for a long time the strongest evidence for <u>continental drift</u> (this is the name for the movement of the large plates of rock that form Earth's crust) were . . . animals!

When scientists studied the fossils of animals that lived on Earth many millions of years ago, they found very similar species on continents that today are separated by wide oceans. The most probable explanation is that these continents were together when these animals walked upon them.

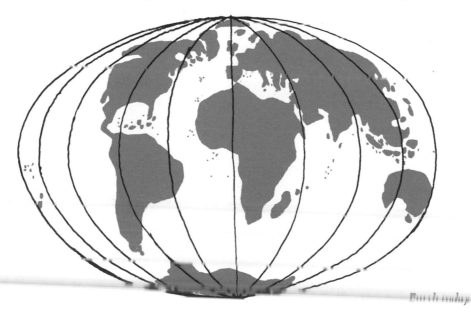

Water dripping day by day wears the hardest rocks away

Even the hardest rocks can't withstand the effect of wind and water passing over them constantly. Over many years, the rocks break apart into small (minuscule) pieces, which are moved to other places. The sand on beaches, for example, is made up of these particles (sometimes mixed with the remains of mollusk shells). This phenomenon of wearing away rock by the elements is called <u>erosion</u>.

The water in rivers and the ocean is one of the main causes of rock erosion. This is why at mouths of rivers we sometimes find large areas of mud: these are sediments carried by rivers along their course that get deposited when the speed of the river decreases as it meets the sea.

One of the most visible forms of erosion caused by water can be seen on sea cliffs. The effect of waves and tides, as well as the wind that blows off the sea, wears the rocks away, forming cliffs and sometimes caves. Larger or smaller pieces fall to the beach and end up getting eroded as well.

Another piece of evidence for erosion by water are river valleys. Notice how the shape of a valley is different according to the part of the river. In the areas farthest upstream (nearest to the source), where the river flows faster, valleys are usually narrower and deeper, while in the areas closer to the river's mouth, where the river flows more slowly, valleys are flatter and more open.

The land around the lowest areas of rivers is generally very rich because of all the sediments carried by the water. This makes these areas excellent for agriculture. It was precisely in these areas that the first human civilizations established themselves. Even today we can see that many big cities are near or on the mouths of big rivers.

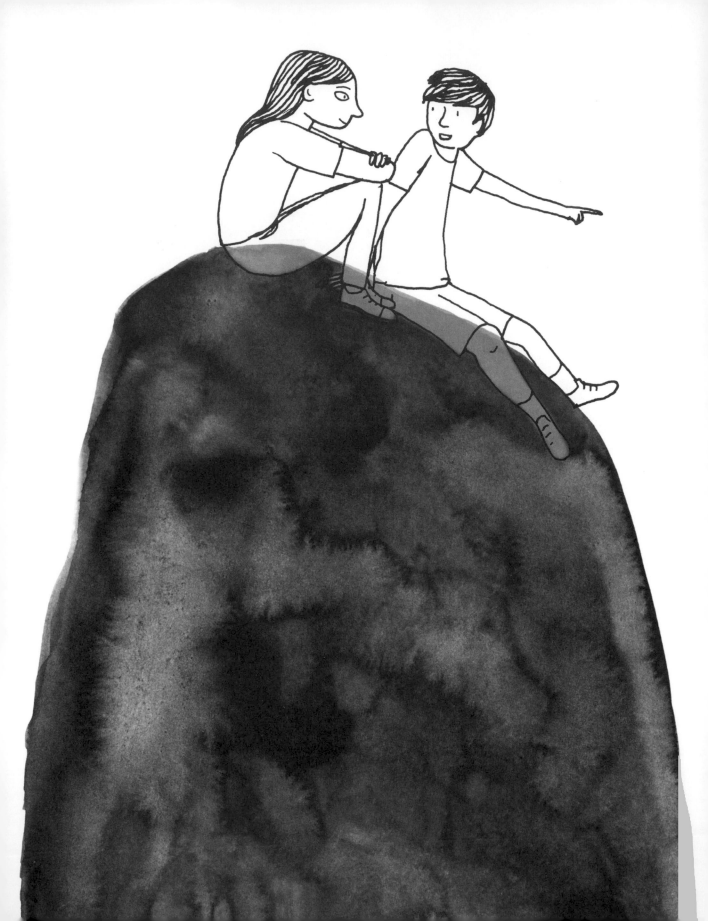

● ● ● ● ●

Collect the many textures of rocks

Use bits of mud or modeling paste to collect the textures of rocks. Press rocks firmly into the soft material, which will mold around the rocks. Look at all the differences!

- - - - - -

Draw with schist

If you happen to walk through an area with lots of schist, look carefully for any (natural) walls of clayish schist where the layers of rock are coming loose. Take a piece and try scratching a flat piece of schist. You'll see how schist can be very soft and will crumble, like chalk, as you write and draw with it.

- - - - - -

Touch rocks with your eyes closed

You can feel the texture of rocks better if you close your eyes. Notice that there are smooth stones (like marble) and others that are very rough (like granite), some that have layers (like schist), some that are very cold, others that are warmer, and some that even have a smell (argillite).

- - - - - -

How many different stones . . .

. . . can you find when you're out for a walk? How about near the ocean? Or on a riverbank?
Make a collection and create an exhibit. Organize a route for visitors and write small labels with whatever information you like. (But don't move big stones from where they are—there might be animals living underneath!)

- - - - - -

A world of grains in the palm of your hand

Sand is made from grains that come from the disintegration of rocks caused by erosion. If you look at a handful of sand, you might see that the grains are all the same—in this case, the sand must be made from a single type of rock. But it's possible that you have lots of different colored grains in your hand—in this case, each grain comes from a different kind of rock. You could be holding bits of the whole world in your hand!

- - - - - -

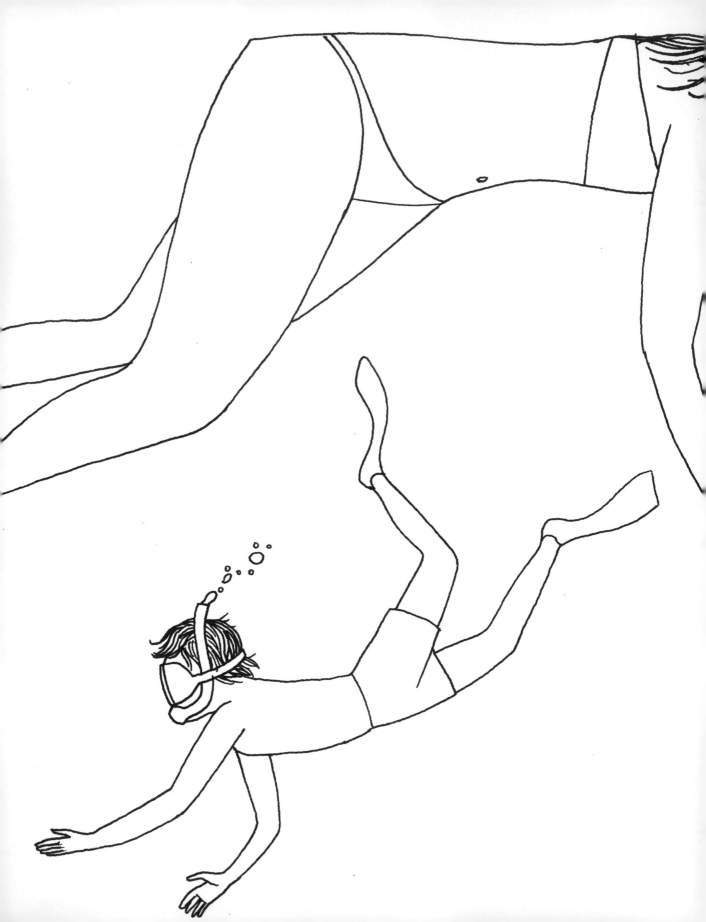

HOW ABOUT WE GO TO THE BEACH?

OCEANS, BEACHES, AND TIDE POOLS

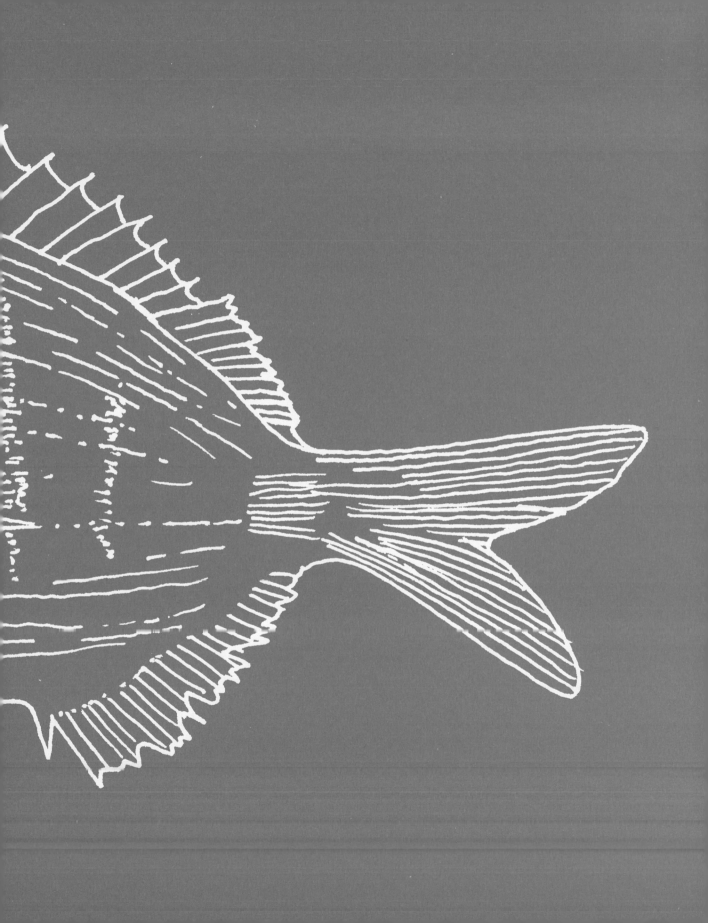

The beach is a very special place, not only because it reminds us of summer vacations, but also because there—with our feet in the sand and the waves arriving every second—we can feel nature in all its force.

Why don't you take your shoes off and come to the beach? There's a lot here to see and learn.

Take a dip with us!

If the water that comes from rivers is freshwater, and rivers flow into the ocean . . . where does the salt in the ocean come from?
As rivers flow over rocks, the minerals that the rocks are made of gradually dissolve in the water. It's these minerals that make salt.

Over the course of millions of years, these small amounts of salt have been carried to the ocean and have accumulated there . . . up to the point that when you get a mouthful of seawater today, there's only one taste it can have: it's very salty!

And why is the ocean blue?
If you look at seawater closely, it's transparent, like the water that comes out of a faucet. So why does it look blue when we see it from a distance?

Some people say it's because the ocean reflects the blue of the sky, which isn't true. The ocean is blue because it mainly reflects blue light, but this effect is only noticeable when there's a large amount of water (especially where the ocean is the deepest).

The different shades of blue that we see are caused by the shadows of clouds, the colors of the seafloor, or by sediments.

Why isn't the beach always the same width?

At many beaches, the ocean is sometimes really far away and we have to walk a long distance to take a dip. This happens because of the tide: when the tide is in, the water comes farther up the beach; when the tide is out, the water stays further away.

Why are there tides?

The sun and moon exert an invisible force on Earth called gravity. However, the moon is closer to us, so it is mostly responsible for tides, pulling the seawater as our planet spins. And this is why when the tide is in at your beach, it is out at the beach on the other side of the ocean.

How do tides work?

Tides work in cycles: as soon as the tide is completely in, it immediately starts to go out again; in a little over six hours, it will be out. Then it starts to come in again, and after another six hours or so, it's in once more.

Spring tides and neap tides

The sun also exerts a gravitational force on Earth, but because it's much farther away, this force isn't as strong as that of the moon. It's still perceptible, though. What happens?

When the sun and moon are aligned (which happens at the full moon and the new moon), the two forces pull in the same direction and the water moves more: these are "spring tides." Then during the first and third quarters of the moon, the sun and moon are not aligned, and they each pull a different direction. (The moon pulls harder because it's closer.) These tides are less strong: they're "neap tides."

The tides are also not the same throughout the year: close to the equinoxes (in March and September) are the strongest spring tides of the year; close to the solstices (in December and June) are the weakest neap tides.

A dictionary for waves

In the world of waves, it's again important that everything has a name and that these names mean the same for everyone.

When you hear someone mention the <u>waterline</u> **(1)**, you know that it's the line that separates the surface of the water from the depths below; the lowest part is called the <u>trough</u> **(2)**; the highest part is the <u>crest</u> **(3)**. The distance between the trough and the crest is called the <u>wave height</u> **(4)**; the distance between two crests or between two troughs is the <u>wavelength</u> **(5)**.

How are waves formed?

The wind blows on the ocean and starts to make very small waves, which make the ocean "rippled." These "<u>ripples</u>"(6) increase the exposed surface of the ocean, which means that more of the wind's energy transfers to the water. The waves gradually gain energy, strength, and height.

When the wind blows in a certain place, the waves that form there start off all jumbled. Then, as the waves leave that area, they become gradually more regular. When we see them arrive at the coast all lined up—the <u>swell</u> (7) that surfers like so much— the waves have traveled several miles.

How do tide pools form?

As the tide goes out, it exposes sand and rocks that minutes before were underneath the water. We call this exposed area <u>intertidal</u>. When this area is rocky, the seawater gets trapped in small holes, forming tide pools.

So do animals get trapped in there? Yes, especially the animals that are stuck to rocks and aren't able to move a lot on their own, like mussels, limpets, anemones, and sea urchins, as well as any that aren't very skilled at walking on land, like fish and shrimp. There are others that like moving from tide pool to tide pool, risking being seen by whoever is passing by—this is the case with crabs and octopuses.

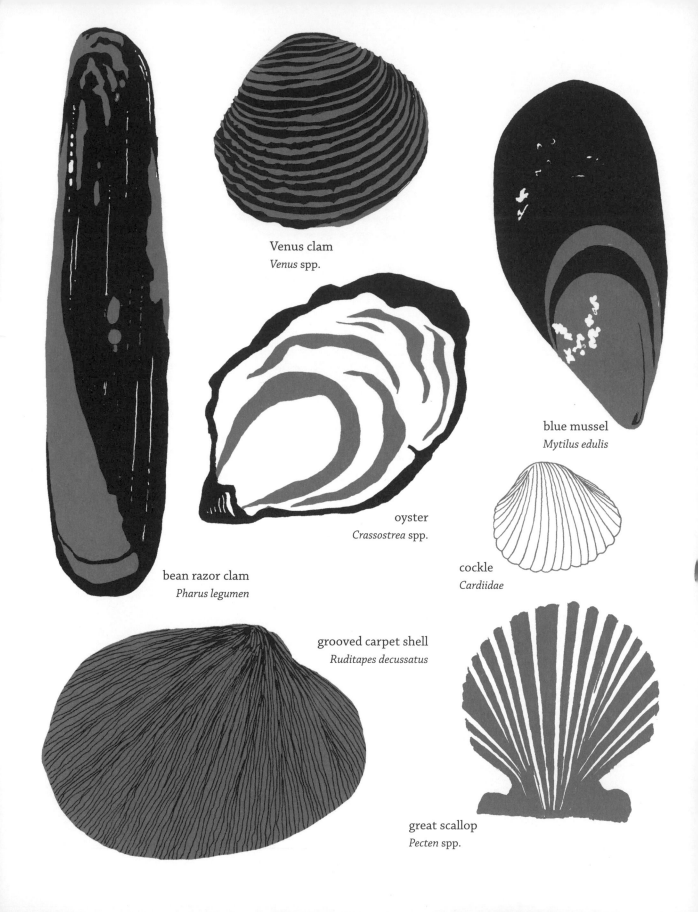

Venus clam
Venus spp.

blue mussel
Mytilus edulis

oyster
Crassostrea spp.

cockle
Cardiidae

bean razor clam
Pharus legumen

grooved carpet shell
Ruditapes decussatus

great scallop
Pecten spp.

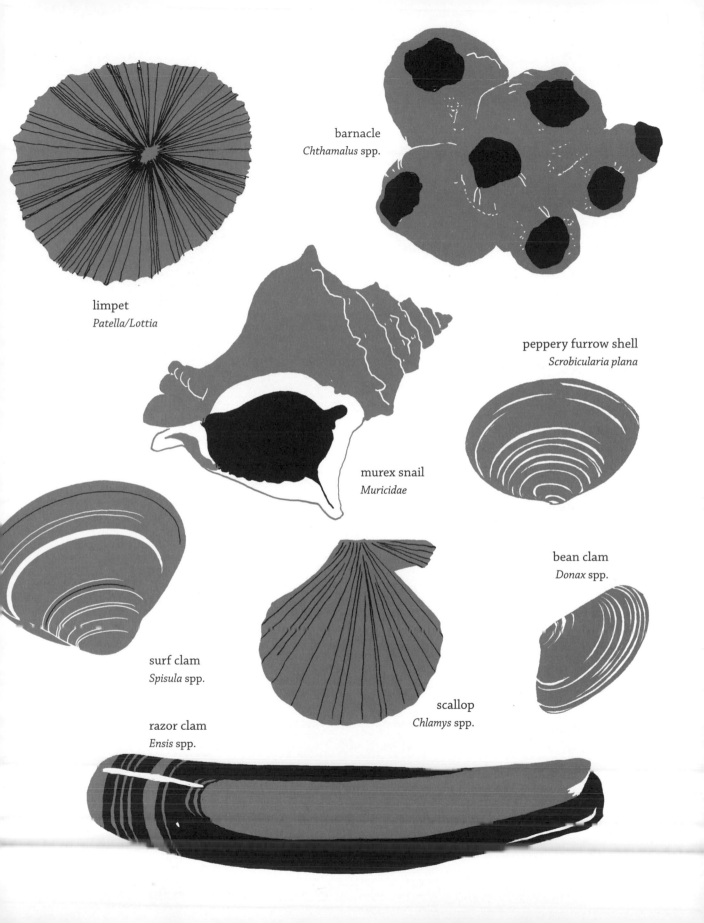

barnacle
Chthamalus spp.

limpet
Patella/Lottia

peppery furrow shell
Scrobicularia plana

murex snail
Muricidae

bean clam
Donax spp.

surf clam
Spisula spp.

scallop
Chlamys spp.

razor clam
Ensis spp.

Do the animals in tide pools eat one another?

Like in any ecosystem, there are predators and prey in a tide pool. But even the hungriest predator doesn't eat everything in front of it. (When you're hungry, you don't eat everything in the fridge all at once!) And don't forget that tide pools are temporary—when the tide comes back in, the animals that were trapped there can finally get out and move somewhere else. What you find in a tide pool can differ a lot from day to day.

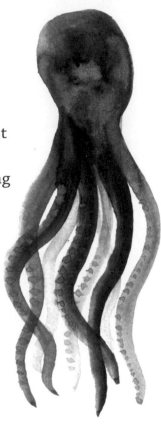

There are real stars in tide pools!

Starfish are the real stars of tide pools. They're pretty, colorful, and—strange as this might seem—they're predators, which means that they hunt other small animals, such as mussels. Plus, they have a peculiar characteristic: when they lose one of their arms, a new one grows back in the same place. But don't pull them off! Their arms take a long time (months, or even years) to grow, and a starfish is more vulnerable to diseases when it loses one.

Another of the "stars" of a tide pool is the octopus. With its eight arms, it can get to all corners of the tide pool, looking for food or escaping from whoever wants to snack on it. Octopuses are very intelligent animals, and they squirt ink to confuse animals that threaten them.

✳

Shall we go tide-pooling?

When biologists make a record of the animals they find in tide pools, it's called a field survey. Even if you're not going to do a scientific study, when you look into each tide pool, you can always learn a lot!

Important tips:
- The seaweed that covers rocks can be slippery. You should also be careful not to cut your feet on shells, so don't go barefoot: it's best to wear an old pair of sneakers (that you don't mind getting wet with seawater).

- Take a net with you to help catch animals and put them in a bucket of seawater for a few minutes. This will make it easier to identify the animals you see, using the pictures in this chapter.

- If you catch an octopus, be careful with the ink! And if you catch a starfish, be careful not to pull off any of its arms.

To "fish" for crabs:
- Some animals in tide pools, like crabs, are able to stay out of the water for a long time. You can try to "fish" them to observe them. To do this, use a net, a bucket, and bait (for example, a piece of mackerel or sardine).

- Go "fishing" at low tide. Look for crabs in the darkest parts of tide pools, underneath laminaria (reddish-brown seaweed) and underneath stones.

- Put bait inside your net. Move the bait slowly and pull gently when the crab bites, but, don't forget, your net should already be in the water to avoid sudden movements!

Warning: It's really important that when you're done, you release the animals back into the tide pool they came from.

Have fun tide-pooling!

301

What's out there beyond the horizon?

When we're at the beach and look out over the ocean, the ocean seems endless. But it does have an end—and this end is another continent. That continent is a very long way away, however, beyond the "curve" of the earth, and that's why you can't see it, even with most powerful binoculars.

Let's go and visit an island

Islands are very special places for biologists because they're sometimes home to species that don't exist anywhere else, and also because lots of marine animals—like seals and seabirds—choose them as a place to breed. Visiting an island with colonies of seabirds or seals is not always easy, but it's not impossible. And it's an unforgettable journey, since it almost always involves a boat ride, during which you can see lots of animals, such as sea turtles, dolphins, or, if you're lucky, a whale.

There are lots of islands that can be easily visited, and the best time to do this is in summer. Depending on the island you visit, you'll be able to find different species.

Gulls are the most common inhabitants, but there can also be terns, petrels and shearwaters. Petrels are rarer and harder to spot—many of them only visit the island during the night (especially on the darkest, moonless nights), to avoid being seen by predators.

If you stay overnight there you might be lucky enough to hear a petrel—some species make an unmistakable sound, and you'll certainly notice if one flies by!

What animals live in the ocean where I swim?

Fortunately, in most places, we don't have to share the ocean with any dangerous animals when we go swimming. But you could stand on a weever or be stung by a jellyfish. But these things don't happen too often, and when we go for a dip, most of the animals around us are harmless. And there are lots of them! Garfish, white seabream, mackerel, and sand smelts, to give just a few examples.

✳ Tips for a different kind of dip

- -

Equipment: A mask, a snorkel, and flippers.

Have you ever tried to open your eyes underneath the water?
If you have, you found out that it's not always easy to see much, and sooner or later, your eyes start to burn because of the salt.

Here are some tips to help you make the most of your dip:
- Get a diving mask so you can see a new underwater world!
- Even better, if you have a snorkel to help you breathe, you can explore without having to come to the surface all the time.
- With flippers, you can swim faster. You'll be able to swim for longer and see more fish, seaweed, anemones, octopuses, and much more.

Warning: Never swim alone! You should always be accompanied by an adult, and never lose sight of them when you're underneath the water. Don't try to catch the animals you find. Some can cause allergic reactions or even bite, so the golden rule is look at everything, but touch nothing!

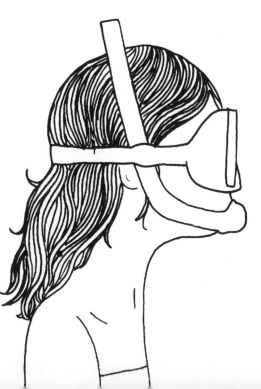

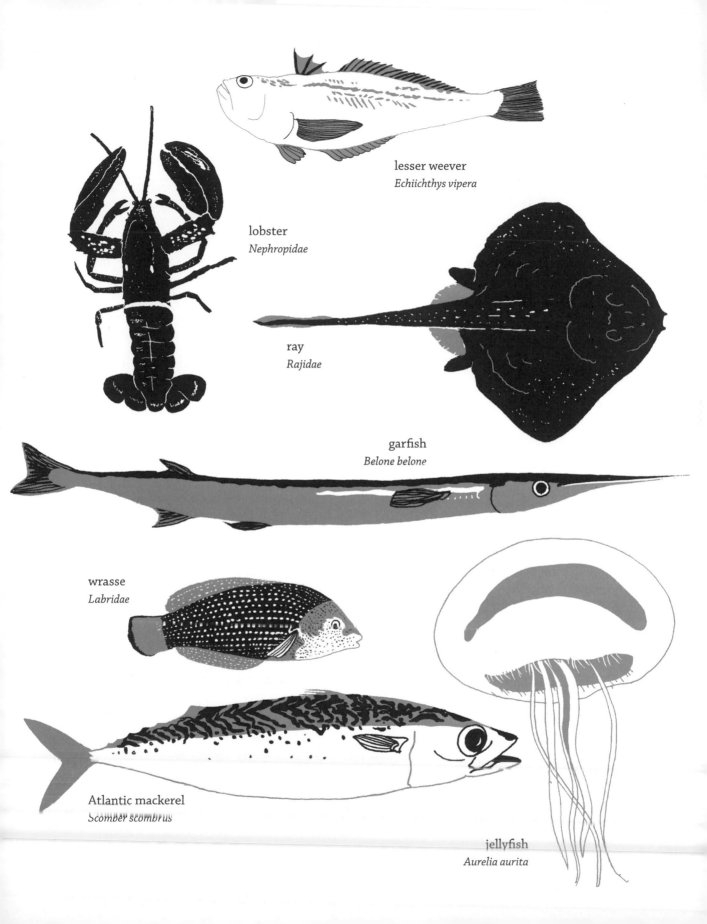

lesser weever
Echiichthys vipera

lobster
Nephropidae

ray
Rajidae

garfish
Belone belone

wrasse
Labridae

Atlantic mackerel
Scomber scombrus

jellyfish
Aurelia aurita

Why don't animals in the ocean drown?
Unlike mammals, which breathe through their lungs, most marine animals breathe through gills (or branchiae), which allow them to breathe the oxygen that is dissolved in water. When the animals are out of the water, they're unable to breathe, because they can't get the oxygen they need to live from the air.

Birds go to the beach, too

Birds also like the beach. They don't go there to sunbathe or swim in the ocean—they go to eat. Buried in the damp sand of low tide or hidden in small tide pools are hundreds of small clams, worms, shrimps, and crabs that serve as food for many species. The birds that often show up for the feast are sanderlings and ruddy turnstones, but you might also see gray plovers, whimbrels, and even purple sandpipers. And, of course, gulls!

And where are all those birds when we don't see them in the summer?
Most of them only like to go to the beach in winter. When spring comes, almost all of them travel to latitudes farther north
(we say they migrate—look again at the chapter on birds),
and they only come back the following autumn.

Coastal birds

There are lots of species of birds that like eating on the mudbanks that are exposed at low tide. When the tide starts to come in they fly away to sheltered areas, where they're protected from the cold, wind, and predators, until the tide goes out again.

Some of these species are well-known to all of us, such as gulls, terns, and sandpipers. Others are less well-known, but that doesn't make them any less beautiful. Estuaries and deltas are excellent places to see them. Find out which is closest to your house and plan a visit. The best times of year are the months of September and May.

ruddy turnstone

herring gull
Larus argentatus

Kentish/snowy plover
Charadrius alexandrinus/nivosus

heron
Ardea spp.

mallard
Anas platyrhynchos

great white egret
Ardea alba

great cormorant
Phalacrocorax carbo

avocet
Recurvirostra avosetta

whimbrel
Numenius phaeopus

sanderling
Calidris alba

spoonbill
Plutulea leucorodia

gray plover
Pluvialis squatarola

black-headed gull
Larus ridibundus

UP IN SPACE!

THE STARS, THE MOON, AND THE SUN

The questions we can ask about the moon and the stars are as infinite as the sky itself. Scientists have managed to find answers for some questions; for others, however, there are only possibilities.

When the sun sets and the temperature drops, there's still a lot waiting for us outside . . .

So put on a jacket, listen to the sounds of the night, and watch the sky.

Let's begin our journey . . .

"Celestial bodies" are everything that exists in space—the moon, the sun, other stars, planets, asteroids, etc.

Because they're closer, the celestial bodies we know best are those in our own solar system. This is where Earth is, spinning around the sun, along with seven other planets.

(1) Mercury (2) Venus (3) Earth (4) Mars (5) Jupiter (6) Saturn (7) Uranus (8) Neptune (9) The Sun

What planets can we see from Earth?

Some planets in the solar system are only observable with the help of a telescope. But others, especially the ones that are closest or biggest, can be seen with the naked eye (i.e., without the help of a telescope), as is the case with Mercury, Venus, Mars, Jupiter, and Saturn.

Because they're between us and the sun, Mercury and Venus can be seen at nightfall and the beginning of the night as well as at the end of the night and daybreak. Venus is the star that is most clearly visible at dusk or dawn—hence, its nicknames the Morning Star and the Evening Star.

To learn to tell a star from a planet, read "Lie in the dark . . . and look at the sky!" later in this chapter.

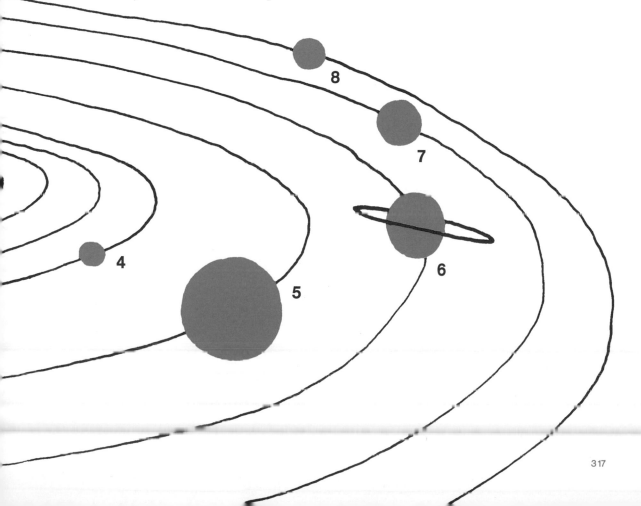

What are stars made of?

Stars are made of the lightest substance in existence: hydrogen.

In the center of a star is a kind of giant cauldron where hydrogen burns throughout the star's life. (Yes, stars are born, and they die, too . . .) The hydrogen turns into another substance called helium, which is a little bit heavier but still very light. (Yes, helium—the same stuff that's used to fill balloons.) Most of the light we receive from stars is produced in these "cauldrons"!

How many stars are there in the sky?

There are small stars, medium stars (like the sun), and giant stars. There are also different colored stars: red ones (which are the coldest), white ones, blue ones (which are the hottest) . . . Scientists don't know the exact number of stars out there, but they do know that there are lots and lots—many more than the grains of sand that exist on all the beaches on our planet.

Why does it look like there aren't any stars during the day?

That's because the light that reaches us from stars is so pale that as soon as the sun appears on the horizon, it blots out all the other stars and makes it look like there's no starry sky during the daytime! But the stars are indeed still there . . .

Go out for a flashlight walk

- - - - - - - - - - - - - -

A flashlight or head-lamp is enough to light your way during a nighttime walk.

If you go with younger brothers and sisters or younger friends, you might want to hold their hands . . . For little kids, the dark can be scary—but also exciting!

Listen to all the nighttime noises. (If you get scared, sing or whistle to yourself.)

Imitate an owl

- - - - - - - - - - - - - -

You can try to get a recording of owls and play it when you're in the countryside. You'll see that other birds will reply to you!

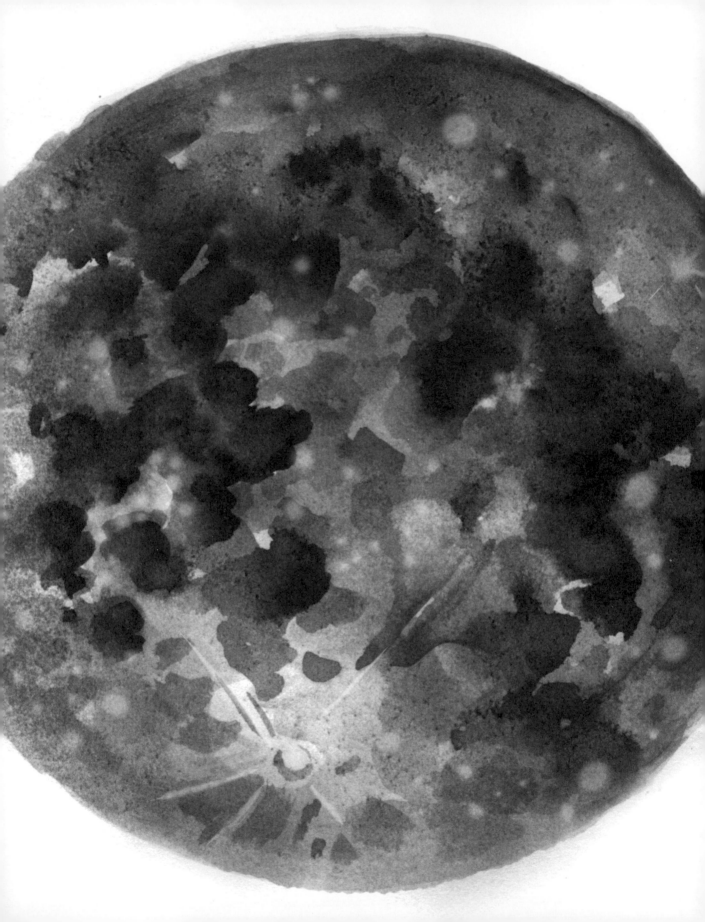

Next stop: the moon

The moon is a sphere almost 2,200 mi (3,500 km) in diameter, and it's Earth's natural satellite, which means it goes around our planet.

What is the moon made of?

The moon formed millions and millions of years ago. It's made of rock, just like Earth, and it might even be Earth's "child"—it could be a chunk of our planet!

This model of the moon's formation proposes that millions and millions of years ago, a very large object hit the Earth, and the impact made bits of our planet fly off. Later, these chunks stuck to the object that hit Earth, and this was the beginning of the new celestial body that began to gravitate around us.

Does the moon have its own light?

The moon isn't a star, and thus, it doesn't emit light. The light we see coming from the moon is called moonlight, and it's actually the light of the sun reflected off the moon's surface.

If you look carefully when the moon isn't full (try using binoculars to do this), you can see the part that isn't lit up by the sun.

Make an animation of the moon!

- - - - - - - - - - - - - - - - -

Using a pad of paper, try to make an animation showing how the moon moves. To achieve this effect (just like in an old-fashioned animation), you have to draw its movement, stage by stage, with each stage on a different page in the pad of paper. When you've finished, flick the pages quickly and watch the moon move: the moon revolving around Earth, Earth spinning, etc.

Note: To help you, look for images on the Internet that show the various stages of the moon.

- - - - - - - - - - - - - - - - -

Why don't we always see the moon?

The moon isn't always visible because it never stays still—it constantly revolves around Earth, taking 27 days and 7 hours to complete a circuit of our planet. While the moon spins around us, we see different areas illuminated by the sun, and there's a period when we can't see the illuminated part because its back is facing us.

An interesting fact: The moon always shows the same side! This happens because its rotation is synchronized—the time it takes to rotate is the same as the time it takes to complete an orbit of Earth.

How fast does the moon move?

The moon moves very fast! The moon orbits Earth at a speed of 2,287 mph (3,683 kph).

Is there life on the moon?

Nope. There are no animals, no plants, and no other kind of living things. As a matter of fact, no form of life has been discovered outside our planet. (Scientists have never found any aliens!)

Even though there's no life there, the moon is very important for the living things on our planet: some animals are more active on nights when the moon is full because they use moonlight to hunt; others only dare to leave their burrows at new moon, in the darkness, so they won't be hunted. Small sea turtles born on the beach use moonlight to find their way back to the ocean. It's also thanks to the moon that there are tides. (Learn why in the "Oceans, Beaches, and Tide Pools" chapter.) And there are lots of animals and plants that need the tides to live.

What kind of moon is there tonight?

On a cloudless night, you can look for the moon in the sky and try to see which phase it's in. Finding the moon might not be easy—if you live in a city, it'd be best to go to an area where you can see a good portion of the sky (in case the moon is hiding behind a building, etc.). If the sky is very cloudy, you can try another day: the moon is much easier to find when there are no clouds.

To identify the phase of the moon, compare it with these images:

New moon
When the moon is between Earth and the sun, the sun only illuminates the side of the moon that "has its back to us." In other words, this is the phase in which it's most difficult to see.

Waxing moon
This is the phase in which the moon is midway between new moon and full moon and is a D shape.

Full moon
When the moon is on the opposite side of Earth from the sun, we see the whole moon illuminated by the sun.

Waning moon
In this phase, the moon is midway between full moon and new moon and is a C shape.

If you can't find a moon at all . . . does that mean it's new moon?

- - -- -- -- -- -- --

Not always. It might just mean that the moon has already set—there's a time when the moon rises and another when it sets (just like the sun). This time changes according to the phase:

o The **full moon** rises at the end of the afternoon and sets in the early morning: you can find it all night.

o The **new moon** rises at dawn and sets at dusk: you can see it, very faintly, during the day.

o The **waning moon** rises at night and sets in the middle of the day, and in the **waxing moon**, the opposite happens.

Lie in the dark . . . and look at the sky!

On a night when there's a new moon, lie on the ground and observe the sky.

As soon as you've gotten used to the darkness, you'll start to see thousands of stars and the odd planet.

Stars twinkle, their light appearing to flicker instead of being constant; planets, on the other hand, don't seem to twinkle and are more "fixed." If you look carefully, it won't take long for you to see some lights slowly crossing the sky, too. These are artificial satellites—devices that orbit Earth and are used for telecommunications, for example. Don't confuse them with "shooting stars," which aren't real stars—they're meteorites. If you're lucky enough to see one of those, don't forget to make a wish!

If you want to know more, take a pocket star guide with you.

Has anyone ever been to the sun?

Nope! They'd be burned to death immediately—the temperature on the surface of the sun is almost 10,000 degrees Fahrenheit (6,000 degrees Celsius). The sun emits light constantly, and this light takes eight minutes to reach Earth. So when we look at the sun, we see it as it was eight minutes ago! This light is the source of energy for all plants and animals on our planet.

Why does the sun rise and set every day?
The sun looks as if it moves in the sky: it rises in the east and sets in the west. But in fact, it's not the sun that moves—it's our planet that moves!

Earth revolves around the sun, but it also spins on its own axis (twirling like a top). Earth takes 24 hours (a whole day) to complete a spin. This movement is called rotation, and the rotation means that the sun illuminates different parts of our planet throughout the day. Earth takes about 365 days to complete an orbit around the sun.

Is sunlight really yellow?

Nope! The sun's light is white because it is made of all the colors of the rainbow. (Did you know that white light is a combination of all colors?) The sun looks yellow to us because the different colors of light don't reach us in the same way—blue and violet stop on the way and "spread out" through Earth's atmosphere—this is why the sky looks blue! The sunlight that reaches us has all the colors mixed together, except the bluish ones, which makes the yellow color that we see.

Why does the sun look much bigger than other stars?

The sun isn't really bigger than all the other stars out there. It's actually medium-sized—there are some stars that are much bigger and others that are much smaller . . . The sun looks bigger than other stars we see at night because it's much closer to us: it's about 90 million miles (150 million kilometers) away. This may seem really far, but the second-closest star to us (Proxima Centauri) is much, much farther away—25 trillion miles (40 trillion kilometers)!

● ● ● ● ● ●

Use the light of the sun (and the shadows it creates)

Let's finish up with some activities that will let you feel the power of the sun and the beauty of shadows . . .

Don't miss sunrise or sunset!

Sunrise and sunset are two of the most magical moments in nature. To see the dawn (sunrise), find a high place, with good visibility and look toward the horizon in the east (the direction in which the sun rises).

To see the dusk (sunset), you'll have to know which way west is.

Look on the Internet to find the exact time of sunrise and sunset in your city.

- -

Paint the sky at sunset

Choose a day when there aren't many clouds. Get everything ready: paints, paintbrushes, paper (or a canvas). As soon as the sun begins to set, start working! Take inspiration from the colors you see.

- -

Check out your shadow

Stretch out a sheet or a piece of paper and stick it on a wall facing the sun. Now step between the sun and the white surface to see your shadow. Get a friend to draw your shadow, and then you can draw your friend's. Don't just stand there—try out funny positions!

Colorful shadows

Use sheets of colored acetate or transparent colored paper to see colorful projections! Just hold up the sheet and see what happens when the sun shines through it and projects a shadow on the ground. You could cut out different shapes of the acetate or paper (for instance, an umbrella or a watering can).

- -

Observe the power of the sun

Sunlight is powerful. Put various materials on a tray (or objects made from different materials). Try a piece of wood, cloth, plastic, rubber, etc. Put the tray in the sun and observe what happens after 1 day, after 5 days, after 10 days, after a month . . .

- -

Draw light and shadow

Look for an area under a tree with light and shade. Move a sheet of paper along the ground to find pretty shapes. When you find some, draw the outlines on the paper.

Note: Never look directly at the sun—it's very dangerous for your eyes.
And don't forget to wear a hat and use sunscreen if you're in the sun for a long time.

The sky offers us unforgettable
sights every day: clouds travel across it,
rain falls from it, the wind blows in it, and
small and large storms form in it . . .

Let's take a good look at it!

What is the sky made of?

The sky is the part of the atmosphere or of space that can be seen from Earth. We say that both clouds and stars are in the sky . . .

What is the atmosphere?
The atmosphere is what we call air.

It's made up of gases, mainly nitrogen (around 78 percent) and oxygen (around 21 percent). There are also smaller quantities of water, dust, pollen . . .

Why doesn't the atmosphere disappear into space?
The atmosphere has a low density and could go on rising constantly until it's lost in the universe. This doesn't happen because the force of gravity keeps it in place, in the same way that it keeps us on the ground.

What's Earth's atmosphere for?
Earth's atmosphere protects living things from the sun's radiation, helps to keep Earth's temperature mild, transports water from one region to another, and contains gases (such as oxygen) that are essential to life.

❋
Try to see the air!

- - - - - - - - - - - - - - -

On a sunny afternoon, find a window where sunlight enters directly. Lie on the floor underneath the window and quietly observe the rays as they enter. Once your eyes get used to it, you'll see that light is reflected off small particles of dust in the air. Sunlight makes these particles visible. Many other particles—which are even smaller—are there as well.

What you've got there is a bit of air, visible air.

- - - - - - - - - - - - - - -

Is there as much air down here as there is up there?

Closer to the surface of Earth, the air is more dense; the farther you get from Earth, the less dense the air is. This means that as we move away from the surface, there is less air. This is why it's harder for us to breathe at the summit of very high mountains!

Does the moon have an atmosphere?

The moon we see from Earth doesn't have an atmosphere because it has very little gravity, but many of the other planets in the solar system and their respective moons do have atmospheres. Even so, none compares to ours!

Why is the sky blue during the day?

The sun emits light of all colors. The mixture of all these colors makes the color white. (This is why we say that sunlight is white.)

During the day, tiny particles in the atmosphere spread out the part of the light that corresponds to the color blue more than others. This is the color that reaches our eyes, which is why the sky looks blue to us.

Rainbows are amazing!

You can see a rainbow when the sun's rays pass through drops of water and are refracted and reflected—the water droplets change the direction of rays of light.

But why do we see rainbows as colors?
Sunlight is made up of all the colors . . . all the colors of the rainbow! But because we normally see all these colors together, we see sunlight as white.

However, when sunlight passes through a drop of water, it's as if the drop is a machine able to separate light into its colors: at that moment, the solar spectrum divides, and all the colors that were previously mixed are visible.

Is it possible to see two rainbows at the same time?
Yes, this does sometimes happen. In these cases, above the main rainbow we see a slightly larger and less bright rainbow. This happens when drops of water reflect the sun's rays doubly.

If you look carefully, you'll notice that the second rainbow has its colors in the opposite order than the first one.

Where should you stand?
To be able to see a rainbow, the sun has to be behind you and there have to be raindrops in the direction you're looking.

✳ Learn the colors of the rainbow

- -

Isaac Newton was the first scientist to manage to separate the colors of sunlight, and back then, he saw only five colors . . . There were other people who saw only six colors . . . Today, though, almost everyone accepts that the rainbow contains seven colors, always in this order: red (on the outside of the rainbow), orange, yellow, green, blue, indigo, and violet (on the inside of the rainbow).

A tip: To learn the sequence of the colors by heart, you can use the acronym Roy G. Biv: imagine a character with that name! The letters also stand for the colors of the rainbow: Red, Orange, Yellow, Green, Blue, Indigo, Violet.

What a lovely nimbostratus . . .

What are clouds?

Clouds are formed by a collection of tiny drops of water or ice crystals. These drops are so small and so light that they float in the air without falling. Clouds become visible in the sky when billions of drops of water group together.

The scientists' code

The system that scientists use to classify clouds was first developed by an English amateur meteorologist, a pharmacist named Luke Howard, in 1803.

In 1887, Ralph Abercrombie and Hugo Hildebrandsson generalized Howard's system, and the system today divides clouds into the following levels of altitude:

<u>High-level clouds</u>
These are the highest clouds, found at altitudes above 4 mi (7 km). Formed of ice crystals, they are fine, white, and shiny, and indicate good weather.

<u>Mid-level clouds</u>
Found at mid-level altitudes, between 1 and 4 mi (2 and 7 km). They're normally in layers, and bluish or grayish in color. They give rise to rain.

Low-level clouds
These are the lowest clouds, found at altitudes of less than 1 mi (2 km).

Vertically developed clouds
The base can be between altitudes of 650 ft and 2 mi (200 m and 3 km).
These clouds can extend upward for up to 6 mi (9 km)!
They give rise to heavy rainstorms.

The 10 types of cloud that exist are grouped into these categories (see the following pages).

Where do the names of clouds come from?
Scientists name clouds using combinations of words that come from Latin:

- Stratus/Strato—flat, crushed, in layers
- Cumulus/Cumulo—bulky, like a cauliflower
- Cirrus/Cirro—fine, curl of hair
- Alto—mid-level
- Nimbus/Nimbo—cloud that brings rain

High-level

<u>Cirrus</u> are the most common high clouds.

<u>Cirrostratus</u> are so fine that they let sun and moonlight pass through.

<u>Cirrocumulus</u> are small, round clouds that look like a thick rope. They appear more in winter and indicate good but cold weather.

Mid-level

<u>Altostratus</u> cover almost the whole sky, and where they are least dense, they let us see the sun like a white disc.

<u>Altocumulus</u> look like little sheep in the sky. If you see them on a warm, humid morning, get ready for a thunderstorm in the afternoon!

Low-level

<u>Nimbostratus</u> have a thick, dark base. When we see them, we might say, "It smells like rain."

<u>Stratus</u> look like mist, but higher. They sometimes give rise to rain showers.

<u>Stratocumulus</u> are gray and fluffy. They rarely give rise to rain.

1 Cirrus

2 Cirrostratus

4 Altostratus

7 Stratus

6 Nimbostratus

3 Cirrocumulus

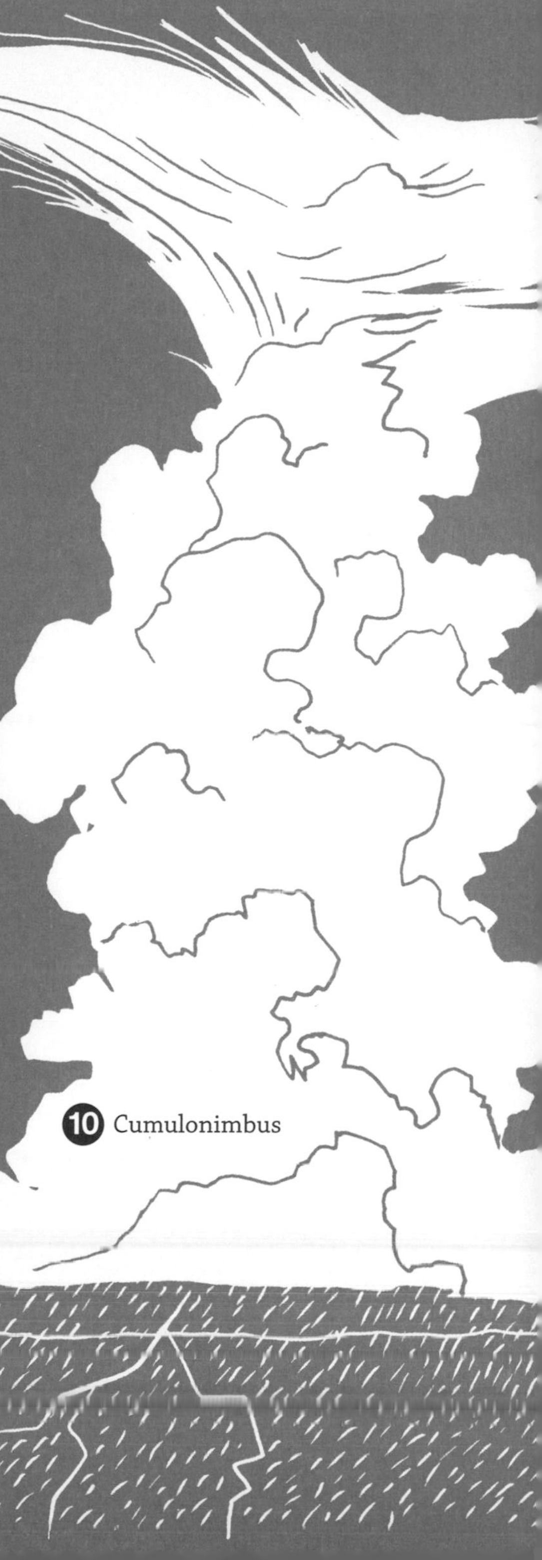

Vertically developed

Cumulus are clouds with a specific shape: the base is flat and the tops are rounded. They're "good weather" clouds, but can easily change . . .

Cumulonimbus are huge clouds that can look like mushrooms. They're known as storm clouds.

Altocumulus

9 Cumulus

10 Cumulonimbus

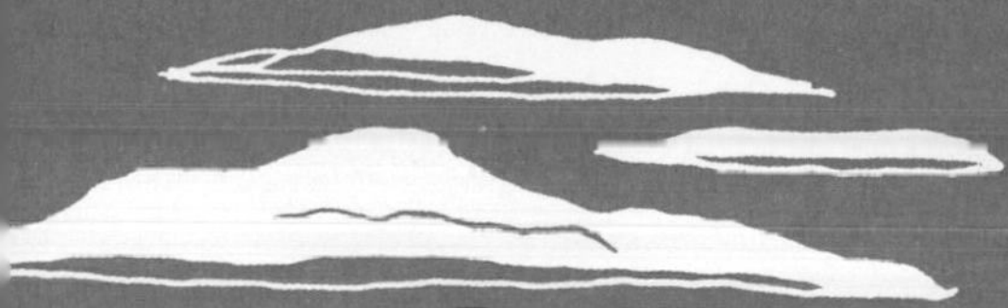

8 Stratocumulus

Here comes the rain!

How do clouds form?

Everyone knows there's water in the air. But water in the air (which you can't see) isn't liquid water—it's water in gas form, or water vapor.

When the air, loaded with water vapor, rises in the atmosphere and meets cold air, the water suspended in it condenses into millions of droplets and forms clouds. These droplets join others, growing bigger and "heavier." And then, ping! It starts raining.

What makes the clouds move?

Clouds are pushed by the wind, of course! The highest clouds are pushed by giant currents of air and can move at over 100 mph (160 kph).

What is wind?

Wind is air that's moving.

And wind is due mainly to the sun's energy. Do you know why?

The sun heats the atmosphere differently in different regions of the planet. These differences in temperature and pressure form wind, with air moving from areas where the pressure is higher to areas where the pressure is lower.

✳ What to do on a rainy day?

- -

Rainy days don't have to be boring!

Here's a list of fun things you can do with a raincoat and pair of rain boots.

Draw the wind
Is the wind visible? Sometimes it is; sometimes it isn't. Can you pin it down on paper using pens or pencils? Try representing it in various ways. Let yourself get carried away by the storm!

Draw animals that fly
There are lots of them: butterflies, mosquitoes, bees, birds (and even fish!).

If you like, you can draw yourself flying among them.

Have a cloud race
Choose a cloud in the sky. Tell your friends to do the same with other clouds. Now watch the wind push your clouds, and see which wins the race!

Jump in a rain puddle!
Only if the puddle isn't very deep, of course— and if you're wearing the right shoes.

Go *splish, splash, splosh* until a grown-up comes along and says: "That's enough!"

You can also try throwing small stones into puddles . . . (No big rocks, though, okay?)

Organize a paper boat regatta
If there's a lot of water running down the street, use one of the streams to organize a race with paper boats. Use pages from magazines: the thicker and shinier the better. Be sure to clean up what's left at the end.

Make rain soup
Put a bucket in the rain until it's full. Then add leaves, stones, flowers, seeds, whatever you find . . . Mix everything with a long stick. What does it smell like?

What does rain do to colors?
Color in several sheets of paper. (You can use pens, colored pencils, or watercolors.) Put the sheets of paper in the rain (on the clothesline, on the porch, in the yard). Look at what happens. You can also get it to rain on a drawing you've already done.

✳

**Go out into the street
on a really windy day**

- - - - - - - - - - - - - - - -

Pick a windy day. Watch how
everything moves: the trees,
the grass, the clothes and
sheets on the clothesline,
people's hair. Close your
eyes and feel the wind
blowing on you.

(If it's cold, make sure to cover
up your head and ears.)

GLOSSARY

Astronomy

The branch of science dedicated to the study of celestial bodies (stars, planets, satellites, galaxies, etc.).

Atmosphere

The layer of gases that surrounds a planet. The most abundant gases in Earth's atmosphere are nitrogen and oxygen.

Biodiversity

The variety and abundance of living organisms that exist in a region.

Blowhole

The respiratory orifice of some marine mammals, which is also used to make sounds.

Botany

The branch of biology that studies plants.

Branchiae

The organs that some animals, such as fish, use to breathe. In fish, these can also be called gills. The larvae of amphibians have branchiae, which they lose when they become adults and develop lungs.

Calyx

The sepals of a flower, which protect the petals and reproductive organs.

Cambium

The layer of tissue that builds xylem and phloem.

Carnivore

An animal that eats other animals.

Cell

The basic structure of living organisms. Animals and plants, for example, are made up of many millions of cells. Cells are so small that they can only be seen with the help of a microscope.

Cocoon

A kind of "wrapper" constructed by the larvae of some insects. The larvae stay protected inside their cocoons while metamorphosis takes place.

Colony (breeding)
A concentration of animals (birds, for example) that make their nests near one another.

Condensation
Passage from a gaseous to a liquid state.

Copulation
Mating to produce offspring.

Corolla
A flower's petals, which normally have the function of attracting pollinators.

D

Deciduous
Used to describe the leaves of plants that fall at a given time of year.

Dioecious
Used to describe a plant that has male and female flowers.

E

Eardrum
A membrane in the ear, which is responsible for the amplification and transmission of sound to the inner ear. Eardrums are frequently visible on amphibians.

Echolocation
The method bats use to detect obstacles, using their hearing. Bats emit sounds that move through space as a wave; when these sounds "hit" an object, they bounce back to the bat's ears. Then their ears pass the information to the brain, which is able to decipher the surrounding environment.

Ecology
The branch of biology that studies the relationships between organisms and the environment that surrounds them.

Ecosystem
The sum of all the organisms that live in a region, the environment that surrounds them, and all their relationships.

Ectothermic
Animals that regulate their temperature through exchanges of heat with the outside world. They are also called cold-blooded animals. Lizards are an example of this.

Endemic species
A species that only exists in a given region and does not spontaneously occur anywhere else.

Endothermic
Animals capable of regulating their temperature through the production of heat inside the body. Humans, as well as all other mammals, are endothermic.

Entomology
The branch of zoology that studies insects.

Estivation
The state of inactivity of some animals during the summer.

Evolution

Changes in the hereditary characteristics of a species that can occur from one generation to another. This process means that species change and diversify over time, adapting to the changing environment and giving rise to others.

Excrement

Feces, or what we might commonly call poop.

Exoskeleton

The external skeleton of certain animals, made of chitin.

Exotic species

A species introduced in a place to which it is not native.

Extinction

The disappearance of a species. We say that a species is extinct when all the organisms in that species have died.

F

Fertilization

The union of male and female reproductive cells, giving rise to an ovum, the beginning of a new living being.

Fossil

The name given to the remains of plants or animals that are found in layers of the Earth from thousands or millions of years ago.

Frugivore

An animal that eats fruit. (Therefore, a fructivore is also a herbivore.)

G

Geology

The science that studies the Earth (the composition of rocks, the evolution of our planet, earthquakes, etc.).

Gland

An organ that produces chemical substances with specific functions in organisms (hormones, for example).

GPS

An abbreviation of *global positioning system*. This is a system that allows us to find our exact location using information sent to artificial satellites orbiting the Earth.

Gynoecium

A flower's carpels, its female reproductive organs. The carpels are formed of stigma, styles, and ovaries and can be free or joined together. The term *pistil* is commonly used to describe a free carpel or several carpels joined together. A flower can have one or many pistils.

Gypsobelum

A kind of "dart" produced by some species of gastropod (snails, slugs, etc.) that is part of their reproductive apparatus. Before copulation, the gypsobelum is introduced into the mate to make it more receptive. This is also called a dart or love dart.

H

Habitat
A location with the conditions necessary for the survival of a species.

Herbivore
An animal that eats plants.

Hermaphrodite
An organism that has both male and female reproductive organs.

Herpetology
The branch of zoology that studies reptiles and amphibians.

Hibernation
The state of inactivity of some animals during winter that allows them to save energy. Some species bury themselves or hide in caves and stay there to sleep for several weeks or months.

Hormones
Chemical substances produced by organisms that circulate inside them (almost always in the blood). One of their functions is to allow organisms to communicate with one another.

I

Ichthyology
The branch of zoology that studies fish.

Inflorescence
The form in which flowers group together on a plant. There are different kinds of inflorescence: raceme, capitulum, amentum, panicle, corymb, umbel, and spadix.

Insectivore
An animal that eats insects. (An insectivore can be considered a special kind of carnivore.)

J

Jurassic
A period in the history of our planet that happened millions of years ago (but precisely between 199.6 and 145.5 million years ago).

L

Larva
The state of some animals before they become adults. Larvae do not reproduce. They can look like adults (as is the case with cockroaches), or they can look very different (as is the case with butterflies).

M

Malacology
The branch of zoology that studies mollusks.

Mammalogy
The branch of zoology that studies mammals.

Marcescent
Used to describe leaves that, even though they are dead, do not fall from the plant

until new leaves begin to grow.

Metamorphosis

A drastic alteration in form that some animals go through (butterflies, for example) when they change from larva to adult.

Meteorology

The science that studies the phenomena that occur in the atmosphere, in particular those related to the weather. (Meteorologists are the people who are able to predict if it will be sunny or rainy tomorrow.)

Mimicry

The ability of animals to change their appearance to match the environment around them and therefore go unnoticed. Chameleons have this ability.

Monoecious

Used to describe a plant that has male and female flowers on the same plant. This is different than a hermaphroditic plant, the flowers of which have both sexes.

N

Native species

A species that exists in a region and was not taken there artificially (i.e., by humans).

Nectar

A sugary liquid produced by flowers that is used to attract pollinators.

Nymph

One of the stages of insect metamorphosis, between larva and adult.

O

Omnivore

An animal that eats both plants and animals.

Ornithology

The branch of zoology that studies birds.

Oviparous

An animal whose offspring develop in eggs, outside the mother. Birds are the most common example.

Ovoviviparous

An animal whose offspring develop inside eggs, inside the mother's body. In other words, the eggs are laid when the offspring are ready to be born.

Ovule

A female reproductive cell.

Ozone

Ozone is a substance that exists in the atmosphere, surrounding our planet like a shield (or layer) that protects us from the most harmful solar rays. It's getting thinner and thinner due to pollution caused by humans. In the places where it is so thin that it lets lots of radiation through, we say there is a hole in the ozone layer.

P

Paratid glands

These are glands in amphibians that produce a milky substance used as defense against predators.

Parthenogenesis

The process by which a female produces an embryo without fertilization taking place.

Pellet

Undigested remains regurgitated by animals; pellets are often used by biologists to study the diet of certain species.

Perennial

A perennial plant has leaves all year round, unlike deciduous plants. A plant is also described as perennial when its life cycle is longer than two years.

Pheromones

Chemical substances that organisms produce and that spread out through the air (or water) to "communicate" with other organisms of the same species.

Phloem

A tissue that transports sap from the leaves to all other parts of a plant.

Phloem sap

A liquid formed of sugars and other nutrients, almost always produced by the leaves of plants.

Photosynthesis

The process whereby plants transform carbon dioxide (from the air) and water (absorbed through their roots) into glucose, with the help of the sun. Glucose is the plant's source of energy.

Pineal eye

An organ that exists on the top of the head of some reptiles (and certain other animals). It is not used to see, but only to give an idea of the light around the animal.

Piscivore

An animal that eats fish. (A piscivore can be considered a special kind of carnivore.)

Pollen

Minute grains produced by the male organs of flowers (stamen) that carry the male reproductive cells. When these cells join with female reproductive cells (ovules), they give rise to seeds.

Pollination

The sexual act of plants, or the passage of pollen from stamen to the gynoecium. When this happens within a flower or between two flowers on the same plant, it is called self-pollination; when it happens between flowers on different plants, it is called cross-pollination.

Pollinators

Elements that help plants carry out pollination. They may be various kinds of animals such as insects, birds, or mammals, or agents that are not living things, such as the wind (anemophily) or water (hydrophily), or humans (artificial).

Population
Organisms of the same species that live in a given area.

Predator
An animal that kills another animal in order to eat it.

Prey
An animal killed by another organism for food.

R

Reproduction
The way living things produce other living things, their descendants, which continue the species. Reproduction can be sexual, when sex cells from two living things (female and male) come together, or asexual, when a single living thing produces another one exactly like it (as in parthenogenesis or when plants grow roots that produce other plants).

S

Scientific name
All species of living things have a scientific name. This is formed of two parts: the first is the genus and must be written with a capital letter; the second is called the species. Both should be written in italics.

Species
A group of organisms that is able to reproduce together and have fertile offspring.

Spermatozoid
A male reproductive cell. When it joins with an ovule, they make a fertilized egg, which then develops into an embryo.

Spiracle
The respiratory orifice of animals such as sharks, insects, and spiders.

Stamen
The male reproductive organs of a flower where pollen is stored.

Suber
The name give in botany to the bark of woody plants. It's the tissue that protects the plant and makes it waterproof.

Subspecies
Different forms of the same species are called subspecies.

T

Tadpole
The form of amphibians when they are young (larvae).

Toxins
Poisonous substances produced by living organisms to defend themselves from predators.

U

Ultraviolet radiation

These are rays of light from the sun (or other stars), but they are different than those that form colors. We aren't able to see ultraviolet rays (unlike other animals such as insects), but their harmful effects are well known—they cause sunburn when we don't protect our skin enough.

V

Viviparous

An animal whose offspring develop inside the mother's body. Mammals are viviparous. (Us humans are, too, because we're mammals.)

Vocal sacs

Skin membranes that many amphibians have in their throats or the sides of their mouths that serve to amplify sound when they want to call a mate or give warnings.

Vulnerable species

A species at risk of extinction. This is one of the eight categories of threat used to classify species. The others are: *Extinct, Extinct in the Wild, Critically Endangered, Endangered, Near Threatened, Least Concern*. This classification is used internationally and is represented in the IUCN (International Union for the Conservation of Nature) Red List.

X

Xylem

The tissue in vascular plants that transports xylem sap from the roots to the leaves.

Xylem Sap

A liquid made from water and mineral salts that, in vascular plants, is transported from the roots to other parts of the plant (generally the leaves) where it will be transformed into sugar.

Z

Zoology

The branch of biology that studies animals.

TIMELINE
IMPORTANT DATES

350 BC (approx.)

The Greek philosopher Aristotle collects examples of fauna and flora to group them according to their characteristics. This is the first classification of living things that we know of.

1632

Birth of Benedict de Spinoza, the philosopher who understood nature as a continuation of God. For Spinoza, stones, animals, and plants all have a body and mind.

1735

The botanist Carl von Linné (known as Linnaeus) publishes the first edition of *Systema Naturae*—the system of classification used, even today, to classify living things according to what we call their scientific name.

1866

Ernst Haeckel first coins the term "ecology" to describe the study of the relationship between organisms and where they live. The word comes from the Greek "logos" (study) and "oikos" (home).

1872

In the United States, a bill is passed by Congress and signed into law by President Grant to create the world's first national park. Yellowstone National Park now comprises more than 2 million acres.

1895

The National Trust is founded in the UK to preserve outdoor spaces and prevent them from being built on. Today they are the UK's biggest land owner.

1915

In the UK, banker and expert naturalist Charles Rothschild holds a meeting to discuss his radical idea about saving places for nature. This meeting leads to the creation of the Society for the Promotion of Nature Reserves (SPNR) and signals the beginning of UK nature conservation.

1915

The Ecological Society of America, a nonprofit organization of scientists, is formed. Within two years, the ESA has 307 members.

1949

The book *A Sand County Almanac*, by Aldo Leopold, considered the father of wild ecology, is published. One of his most famous quotes is that we must learn to "think like a mountain."

1960

The British scientist James Lovelock proposes a theory known as the Gaia hypothesis, in which he presents the Earth as a unique living organism that is able to regulate itself in many ways.

1962

The biologist Rachel Carson publishes the book *Silent Spring*, in which she shows the risks of unregulated use of pesticides (DDT), especially to birds. This book led to a revolution in environmental laws.

1970

Earth Day is celebrated for the first time, on the April 22, in the United States.

1970

The European Council launches the European Year of Nature Conservation.

1971

Two of the world's most important environmental association are created: Friends of the Earth International and Greenpeace.

1973

Arne Naess introduces the concept of "deep ecology." For this Norwegian philosopher and mountaineer, nature is not just something to be manipulated for our benefit; it is a place for us to share, equally.

1973

The Convention on International Trade in Endangered Species of Wild Fauna and Flora (CITES) is approved, prohibiting the sale and purchase of thousands of endangered species.

1987

Introduction of the concept of "sustainable development," which demonstrates that the economy, people, and the environment must be linked, bearing the needs of future generations in mind.

1992

In Rio de Janeiro, world leaders meet to discuss the planet's environmental situation (at a conference known as ECO 92).

1997

Year of the Kyoto Protocol, which lays out goals for the reduction of global greenhouse gases, which are responsible for global warming.

2007/2009

The General Assembly of the United Nations dedicated the period between 2007 and 2009 for commemorations of International Year of Planet Earth.

2010

The United Nations declares 2010 International Year of Biodiversity.

If you want to know more . . .

Here are some organizations that work in the area of nature conservation or study. Check the websites to learn more about their activities:

Worldwide:

BGCI Botanic Gardens Conservation International
○ www.bgci.org

BirdLife International
○ www.birdlife.org

Conservation International
Environmental organisation
○ www.conservation.org

Earth Island Institute
○ www.earthisland.org

Earthwatch Institute
○ earthwatch.org

International Union for Conservation of Nature
○ www.iucn.org

Oceana
○ na.oceana.org

The Nature Conservancy
○ www.nature.org

UNEP-WCMC United Nations Environment Programme
○ www.unep-wcmc.org

UNESCO United Nations Educational, Scientific and Cultural Organization
○ en.unesco.org

WCS Wildlife Conservation Society
○ www.wcs.org

WWF World Wide Fund for Nature
○ www.worldwildlife.org

In the US:

AMNH American Museum of Natural History
○ www.amnh.org

National Audubon Society
○ www.audubon.org

NPCA National Park Conservation Association
○ www.npca.org

NPS National Park Service
○ www.nps.gov

SCA Student Conservation Association
○ www.thesca.org

USGS United States Geological Survey
○ www.usgs.gov

In Australia and New Zealand:

ACF Australian Conservation Foundation
○ www.acfonline.org.au

Government of South Australia Department of Environment, Water and Natural Resources
○ www.environment.sa.gov.au

NZ Department of Conservation
○ www.doc.govt.nz

Parks Australia
○ www.parksaustralia.gov.au

In the UK:

BSBI Botanical Society of the British Isles
○ www.bsbi.org.uk

Friends of the Earth
○ www.foe.co.uk

Greenpeace
○ www.greenpeace.org.uk

JNCC Joint Nature Conservation Committee
○ www.jncc.defra.gov.uk

The National Trust
○ www.nationaltrust.org.uk

RSPB Royal Society for the Protection of Birds
○ www.rspb.org.uk

The Wildlife Trusts
○ www.wildlifetrusts.org